The Schools of Ba'athism

A Study of Syrian Schoolbooks

Meyrav Wurmser

Arabic Translations by MEMRI Staff

The Middle East Media Research Institute
A MEMRI Monograph

Washington, D.C.

© 2000 by the Middle East Media Research Institute

Published in 2000 in the United States of America by the Middle East Media Research Institute, 1815 H Street, NW, Suite 404, Washington, D.C. 20006.

ISBN 0-9678480-0-8

Cover Design by Debra Naylor, Naylor Design Inc.

About the Author

Dr. Meyrav Wurmser is the Executive Director of the Middle East Media Research Institute (MEMRI). She received her Ph.D. from the George Washington University in Washington, D.C. She has taught at the Johns Hopkins University and the United States Naval Academy. She has written numerous articles about Israel, the Arab world, and Zionism. Her article "Can Israel Survive Post-Zionism?" was the lead article in the March 1999 issue of *Middle East Quarterly*.

MEMRI is an independent, non-partisan, non-profit organization. MEMRI was established in February 1998 to study and analyze intellectual developments and politics in the Middle East and the Arab-Israeli conflict, with a particular emphasis on issues relating to the peace process. In its research, MEMRI is dedicated to the proposition that the values of liberal democracy, civil society, and the free market are relevant to the Middle East and to United States foreign policy toward the region.

Contents

Acknowledgments

The author wishes to express her deepest gratitude to several individuals without whom this publication could not have been written. In particular, they include Yotam Feldner, Aluma Solnik, and Eli Carmeli, who translated the Syrian textbooks from Arabic; Brendan Wilson-Barthes and Aaron Mannes, in MEMRI's Washington office, who assisted in all the different stages of this project; Yigal Carmon and Dr. Hillel Fradkin, who gave invaluable suggestions and helped conceptualize this work; Dr. Cheryl Weissman, who edited the manuscript; and Dr. David Wurmser, whose thoughtful suggestions, good humor, and kind encouragement accompanied this volume since its conception.

Foreword

Since 1991, the United States has spent a great deal of time and political capital (and perhaps potentially money) in trying to bring about an Israeli-Syrian peace accord. Such an accord would take Syria (and its Lebanese proxy) out of the camp of Arab states hostile to Israel.

But a long-lasting peace between Israel and Syria will require more than just a signed document, as important as that may be. Peace must be translated into the realities of friendly, mutual cooperation between the two peoples. That will entail a major change in Syria's traditionally hostile attitude toward Israel, an attitude with which the regime has been indoctrinating its youth for decades. As the peace process and the U.S. efforts to foster it continue, we will have to learn more about the changes that Syrian society must undergo if peace is to come to the region.

Changes in a society can occur on various levels: in the media; among the elite, especially in the cultural sphere; in the legislature; and so forth. The most important change, however, must take place in the educational system, from elementary school to the universities.

This study of Syria's government-run educational system, through its textbooks and its curriculum, opens a previously closed window into the bleak reality of institutionalized hatred not only against Zionism and Israel, but also against "the Jews" in general. That enmity is expressed through a systematic campaign to delegitimate Israel and to present it as a dangerous threat to the Arab world. The means advocated by the textbooks to deal with that danger are *Jihad* [holy war] and martyrdom against Israel and the Jews. The harsh images evoked by the schoolbooks include not only direct calls for suicide attacks against Israel, but also anti-Semitic portrayals of the unchange-able, treacherous nature of the Jews throughout history.

Those ideas and beliefs, which the Syrian educational system works to instill in the minds of its children and youth, reflect the ideological world that guides the Syrian state and society. The hatred toward Is-rael and the Jews that is found in Syrian schoolbooks is much more than a passing phenomenon, because it is just one specific expres-sion of a broad Syrian worldview. The importance of this study lies both in its revelation of that worldview, as expressed in the Syrian educational system, and in its presentation of some of the many diffi-culties that still face all attempts to bring about a true Syrian-Israeli reconciliation.

This study could not have been written without the generous help of Mr. Melvin Cohen. MEMRI and its staff are grateful for his moral as well as material support.

Dr. Munr Kazmir   Yigal Carmon
Chairman   President

Executive Summary

A nation's textbooks show how that nation views its past, present, and future, what it admires in its heroes, and what it values and holds dear.

The possibility of a Syrian-Israeli accord raises the question of what changes each society will be required to make in order to achieve true reconciliation with its former adversary. One of the most crucial elements of such a change, underpinning the possibility of normalized relations between the two countries, is the degree to which children are educated to peace in each of the societies. The education of children is, first, a gauge by which to assess the degree of change a society must undertake and, second, an accurate indicator of that society's prevalent view of its adversary, that adversary's motivations, and the conflict between the two states. It provides a unique and clear window into the ideology and worldview that inform a state, its public opinion, and many of its actions.

This monograph examines how Israel, Zionism, and the Arab-Israeli conflict are depicted in some forty Syrian textbooks for children between the fourth and eleventh grades. These books are all part of the official Syrian curriculum and are exclusively authored and used by the state-run educational system. The subject matter they cover includes history, national (pan-Arab) education, geography, literature, social education, and Islamic education. The selection of books and subject matter was directed by the extent to which these texts deal with Israel, Zionism, and the Arab-Israeli conflict.

The key findings of this examination reveal a total rejection of Israel and Zionism in the Syrian curriculum that not only condemns Israel but, what is more disturbing, calls for and indoctrinates the young to take anti-Israel action. Syrian textbooks engage in a broad campaign to delegitimate Zionism. Children learn that Zionism is colonialism, that it is based on fabrications, that it is similar to Nazism, and that it is the ultimate racist movement that inspired Nazi thought and action. The schoolbooks instill in their students the conviction that Zionism endangers the Arab world in its entirety and is the ultimate contradiction to Arab nationalism and its dream of Arab unity. Since pan-Arab ideology underpins the Syrian Ba'athist regime, the notion that Israel's existence prevents Arab unification turns Israel into the archenemy of the Arabs in general and the Syrians in particular. Israel's very existence, within any borders, affronts the essence of Ba'athist ideology and the raison d'être of the Syrian Ba'athist regime. Peace with such an enemy is, naturally, impossible, because any compromise with or recognition of Israel would entail the collapse of the ideological essence of the Syrian state.

The textbooks further depict Israel as an aggressive and expansionist enemy, one that is singularly responsible for the backwardness of the Arab world. As such, it is not only an omnipotent and frightening presence in the region but it has the ability to determine the internal condition of the Arab world.

The inevitable conclusion is that for reasons of ideological and physical Syrian self-preservation, that enemy must be fought to its destruction. Syrian children, therefore, are taught that they must act to remove that threat to the Syrian state and obstacle to Arab unity through *Jihad*—a Muslim religious concept meaning "holy war"—and martyrdom. Even young children are not spared this frequent indoctrination. The schoolbooks promise rewards to those children who agree to commit themselves to strive for martyrdom, for the sake of the great national cause; they threaten those who do not.

Children are taught that they must wage *Jihad* against Israel, despite the fact that the Ba'ath ideology is secular as a matter of principle. Here, the Syrian regime comes to terms with the Islamic roots of most Syrians, utilizing those roots within its educational system to strengthen the willingness of its youth to sacrifice themselves for the Arab cause, as the Ba'ath ideology perceives it.

Beyond inflaming deep religious sentiments and using them in the context of the Arab-Israeli conflict, the Syrian educational system expands hatred of Israel and Zionism to anti-Semitism directed at all Jews. That anti-Semitism evokes ancient Islamic motifs to describe the unchangeable and treacherous nature of the Jews. Its inevitable conclusion is that all Jews must be annihilated.

The Syrian educational system progressively moves from delegitimating Israel, to calls for action against Israel, to calls for the destruction of all Jews. That eternal declaration of war goes far beyond the limits of the Arab-Israeli conflict. It means that the very foundations of Syrian society will have to be changed if peace and normalization are to come to the Middle East.

1

Introduction

One of the focal points of the current negotiations between Israel and Syria, which began on December 15, 1999, is the future relationship between Israeli and Syrian societies. Peace between the two peoples involves normalization of relations. The Israeli position is that open and warm relations between the two peoples can guarantee the longevity and stability of the peace. That will require an acceptance of Israel by Syria and its public.

Syria might eventually accept that position. But if it does, a change in the relations with Israel will entail a great ideological change. It is clear that if Israel is to gain the normalization of relations it is seeking, the Syrian regime will have to overcome an enormous obstacle of its own making: the delegitimation of Israel in Syrian society. Israel's total delegitimation is a central tenet not only of the documents of Syria's ruling party, the Ba'ath, and the pronouncements of its leaders, but also of the Syrian educational system. It is an integral part of the schooling of Syrian children, as reflected in their current textbooks. All Syrian children between the early years of elementary school and the upper levels of high school are directly exposed to anti-Semitic, anti-Israel, and anti-peace messages.

Ba'athism, the codified ideology of Syria, is not just a theoretical construct that occupies the minds of a few party intellectuals. Since Syria obtained its independence in 1945, the military wing of the

Ba'ath Party took part in many of the coups that have been a feature of modern Syrian history. Army officers, as the core constituency of the party, endorsed the new ideology. In the 1960s, the Ba'athist Party gained full control of the state, and its ideology became dominant. Thus, Arab nationalism, as defined by the Ba'ath Party founders, served both as the ideological legitimacy and the raison d'être of the Syrian regime. Upon taking power, the regime subordinated the school structure, and especially the curriculum, to shaping young Syrians to properly understand and internalize Arab nationalism as defined by its ideology.

The identification between the Syrian state and the Ba'ath Party is apparent in the textbooks quoted in this study. They are written and published exclusively by the Ministry of Education, and they quote long passages from the party's indoctrination books.[1] Hence, the Syrian school system serves as an extension of the Ba'athist indoctrination structure and provides fertile ground to inculcate children with the ruling party's line.

Since the issues of Zionism and the state of Israel feature prominently in Arab nationalist thought, and especially in Ba'athism, it is no surprise that Syrian textbooks also deal extensively with them. The attitudes reflected in these texts are totally negative toward Israel and Zionism. A principal theme of their anti-Israel lessons relates to the Palestinian-Israeli conflict. Israel is viewed as an illegitimate political entity because of what the textbooks describe as its theft of Palestine and its expulsion and massacre of the Palestinians.

But the critique of Israel in the Syrian curriculum goes far beyond the Palestinian-Israeli issue—so much so that solving the Palestinian-Israeli conflict would not remove the traditional Ba'ath objection to the legitimacy of Israel. Israel is a menace not only to the Palestinians, according to Syrian textbooks, but to the Arab nation as a whole. That is because Israel is an expansionist entity that disrupts Arab unity, divides the Arab world, and causes its backwardness.

That view of Israel is crucial to the identity and self-understanding of the Ba'athist Syrian regime. Ba'athism, created in Syria during the 1940s under the leadership of two Arab intellectuals, Michel 'Aflaq and Salah Al-Din Al-Bitar, comprises three principal ideas: unity, freedom, and socialism. It advocates a synthesis between Arab nationalism and revolutionary socialism within an all-Arab state, stretching from the "Arab" Gulf in the East to the Atlantic Ocean in the West.[2] That ideology—which negates the basic Western concept of individualism—emphasizes the principle of collectivity in a unitary "Arab nation." As Michel 'Aflaq wrote:

> Imagine a man whose nationalism has not yet been awakened. . . . What sort of a person would he be? What would history mean for him? . . . Whenever I think of the situation of such a person, I shiver with fear at the thought of the misery and isolation he may suffer.[3]

The concept of Arab unity means that the Syrian regime strives to transcend the Syrian state and replace it with a union of all Arabs. Arab nationalism, therefore, is a supranational idea that conflicts with Western notions of liberal-nationalism and patriotism. The Ba'ath teach that only when the Arabs unite will they restore their past grandeur as one of the world's leading civilizations.

The concept of freedom, according to 'Aflaq, entails fighting against colonialism. The whole of Arab civilization is engaged in a total struggle against the imperialism and colonialism that represent Western civilization. In that battle, disunity is bound to bring defeat to the Arabs. As the Ba'ath Party's 1973 constitution states,

> The Arab nation played a tremendous role in the development of human civilization, when it was a united nation. But when the bonds of its national unity weakened, so did its civilizational role which enabled waves of imperialist invasions to tear its unity, occupy its land, and rob its wealth.[4]

Israel, according to Ba'athist ideology, is the agent of the colonialist West in the Middle East. The West created the Zionist movement in order to defeat and control the Arab world. The state of Israel still impairs the Arab world, by physically dividing it and by preventing its unity. That means that Israel constitutes a constant danger to the Arab world, its identity, and its self-definition. As the Syrian constitution explains,

> Any achievement that will be reached by any part of the Arab world will remain incomplete and vulnerable unless it is protected by Arab unity and every danger posed by imperialism and Zionism to one Arab state is at the same time a threat to the whole Arab nation.[5]

Thus, for Ba'athist ideology, Israel's very existence explains the failure of the Arab world to unite. Therefore, in order to arrive at its glorious destiny, the Arab nation must erase Israel. The conflict with Israel is existential; either Israel or a united Arab nation, as the Ba'athists understand it, will prevail and survive. And since the pursuit of unity for the Arab nation is the basis for the Syrian regime's claim to legitimacy, the measure of its own ideological success is tied to its ability ultimately to defeat Israel.

For that reason, reconciliation with Israel would shake the ideological foundations of the Ba'athist regime. And that fact would have current, operational implications. It sheds light on the surprising statements made on the White House lawn by the Syrian foreign minister, Faruq Al-Shara, during the Syrian-Israeli talks that began on December 15, 1999. Al-Shara noted that peace would force Syria into a profound reexamination of its ideological underpinnings, especially on the question of Arab unity—the primary pillar of Ba'athist ideology. Accepting Israel as a legitimate state would mean the end of the Ba'athist dream of Arab unity.

This study, which is based on an examination of about forty textbooks for children between the fourth and eleventh grades, reveals how young Syrians are educated to think about the problem of Israel and Zionism. The following chapters reflect the various themes stressed by the textbooks. Chapter 2 analyzes how Syrian schoolbooks present Israel. Zionism is portrayed as a form of colonialism, inherently hostile to the anti-colonial aspirations of the Arab world. Furthermore, it is a movement that lacks any claim to legitimate nationalism. The textbooks also expose children to the Ba'athist idea that Zionism is in fact related to Nazism, and that it is a form of racism.

Chapter 3 focuses on how the Ba'athist state, as revealed in the textbooks, teaches its students to understand the "danger" that Zionism poses. Israel's location, embedded in the heart of the Arab world, physically divides that world, obstructing the achievement of the main goal of the Arab nation—unity. Since the need to rectify that division forces Syria, led by the Ba'ath Party, into conflict on behalf of the Arab nation, it demands of its citizens great sacrifices and severe hardships. In the context of the threat that Israel poses to the Arab nation, and of Israel's inherently negative and aggressive characteristics, the history of the Arab-Israeli wars is recounted to Syrian children.

Chapter 4 examines the way the children are taught to understand the Palestinian question in the framework of Ba'athist ideology. Interestingly, despite the fact that Ba'athism is focused on Arab unity, Syrian children are educated to advocate an independent Palestine.

Chapter 5 deals with peace and struggle. Syrian children are taught that real peace with Israel is treason, because its price would be the destruction of the Arab nation and the freedom of Arabs. Hence, the Syrian curriculum advocates the merits of continuous struggle.

Chapter 6 reveals the means that the Syrian educational system believes should be used in the permanent struggle against Israel. If peace is impossible and eternal struggle against Zionism inescapable, how then is such a war to be waged, and what role should children play in it? Ba'athism is a secular ideology, yet the intellectual structure through which a Ba'athist state demands the sacrifices, or even deaths, of its students relies on Islamic religious beliefs and justification. Chief among those beliefs is the duty of Muslims to wage *Jihad* [holy war] against Israel. In being taught that it is their personal duty to strive for martyrdom, Syrian children learn to embrace, even relish, death through martyrdom. As part of their education for accepting death, children are also taught of the virtues and benefits of martyrdom. The textbooks include numerous stories of heroism and of the happiness felt by martyrs and their families.

Finally, Chapter 7 exposes the anti-Semitic elements in the Syrian curriculum. In stressing the treacherous nature of Jews, Syrian textbooks borrow from traditional anti-Semitic myths and images. In so doing, they seek to establish the irredeemable and insidious character of the Jews as a people. Here the schoolbooks go beyond the issues of Israel and Zionism, broadening the cycle of hostility to include the Jewish people everywhere. What began as a description of Zionism and Israel as illegitimate phenomena ends with a call to exterminate the Jews.

Notes

1. See, for example, *National [Pan-Arab] Socialist Education for the Eighth Grade, 1999–2000*, p. 16.

2. The socialist element in the Ba'ath ideology has little to do with the economic determinism of Marxism or Leninism. That is because the Arab nation

required national unity, rather than an internal class conflict. As Michel 'Aflaq wrote: "The class struggle in the Arab countries is not just a matter of workers versus capitalists; it is also the Arab masses versus all opponents of Arab unity." Quoted in David Roberts, *The Ba'ath and the Creation of Modern Syria* (London & Sydney: Croom Helm, 1987), p. 68.

3. Michel 'Aflaq, *On the Path of the Ba'ath* (Beirut, 1963), p. 48.

4. *Al Thawra* (Damascus), February 1, 1973.

5. Ibid.

2

Delegitimating Zionism

Syrian textbooks engage in a systematic campaign to delegitimate Israel and the Zionist ideology upon which it is based. As part of that campaign, they portray Zionism as the close ally of a colonialist/imperialist West, still viewed as the key nemesis of the Arab nation. The delegitimation does not stop there: according to their portrayal, Zionism has so integrated itself with the West as to have become (if it was not always) a colonialist movement.

Moreover, claim Syrian textbooks, Zionism is illegitimate because it fabricated a connection between the Jewish people and the land of Israel that did not exist. The books further attempt to erode Zionism's legitimacy by attaching to it the stigma of two abhorrent beliefs: Nazism and racism.

Zionism as Colonialism

Syrian textbooks depict Zionism as "the single most dangerous movement opposing Arab nationalism, whose goal is to destroy Arab existence and to settle world Jewry in Arab Palestine with the assistance of colonialism."[1] The books describe the rise of Zionism in the nineteenth century as resulting from an alliance between the Jews and the colonialist powers, especially Great Britain. That alliance was natural, they claim, because a commonality of interests existed between covetous Zionist ambitions and British colonialist designs for Palestine.[2]

7

According to a textbook for the tenth grade, the leaders of the Zionist movement in the nineteenth century realized that a Jewish state could be created only with the support of the great colonialist powers. Therefore, Zionists had to claim that they too were colonialists—that they were Europe's agents in the Middle East.[3] Zionism would assist in ridding Europe of its unwanted Jews.[4] The charge that Zionists were agents of colonialism, appearing twice in the tenth-grade schoolbook, is derived from a quotation from the creator of Zionism, Theodore Herzl. He observed that Zionism would establish in Palestine a fortress for Europe against Asia and a front-line base for culture against barbarity.[5] According to Syrian textbooks, Zionism is a tentacle of European colonialism, designed to rob the Arab world of its unity, its culture, and its inheritance in Palestine. Another textbook, written for eighth-graders, illustrates that point in the following passage by claiming that Israel is the vanguard of European culture in the Middle East:

> The world became familiar with the message of civilization and development that Israel introduced into the Arab area through the mass expulsions and massacres of the citizens, the prison camps, the demolition of Arab houses, the plunder of lands, the bombing of citizens and their mass murder, starting with Deir Yassin and ending with Kfar Kana.[6]

The colonialist powers, maintains the same book, supported the Zionist enterprise for reasons that included carrying out their schemes to gain control over the Arab homeland, ridding themselves of their Jews, and maintaining Jewish loyalty even after the immigration to Palestine. That was because the Jews—according to old anti-Semitic lore—were said to be a very powerful and influential group worldwide.[7]

The schoolbooks provide variations on the theme. A later chapter in the same eighth-graders' textbook informs the reader that the colonialist powers cooperated with wealthy Jewish businessmen, who were searching for new markets for their investments, to create the Zionist movement in the nineteenth century. The textbook explains:

> After the rise of colonialism and the European states' takeover of many of the lands in underdeveloped countries, some thinkers among the rich Jews, together with the colonialist states, wanted to create an entity

ments for them. They had their mind set on settling in the land of Palestine, which would be a starting point for them in order to take over [the entirety of] the Arab homeland, to rob its treasures and to convert it into a site in which their money could be invested. In order to accomplish this, a movement called "the Zionist movement" was established.[8]

That account of the creation of the Zionist movement not only portrays it as an ally of the evil colonialists, but also echoes two additional ideological frameworks incorporated into the Syrian worldview. The first has to do with classic anti-Semitism. *The Protocols of the Elders of Zion* (1905), one of the leading anti-Semitic works of modern times, describes a world run by an all-powerful, international, secret committee of Jews who cooperate in order to protect Jewish interests. Similar to the *Protocols*, the Syrian tenth-grade textbook describes Zionism's origin not as an authentic national movement but as a scheme hatched by wealthy Jews who were powerful enough to influence the policies of the world's leading colonialist powers.

The second ideological framework reflected in the text has to do with Vladimir Ilich Lenin's writings. Revolutionary socialism is a key component of the Syrian Ba'ath Party's ideology, which also includes a radical Arab nationalist element. In his well-known *Imperialism, the Highest Stage of Capitalism* [1916], Lenin explained that capitalist nations reach a point of crisis, at which their markets become saturated.[9] To resolve that crisis, those nations turn imperialist and start conquering weaker and poorer nations (as the British did to India), which provide them with new markets for their goods, cheap labor, and a source of raw materials. Similarly, the explanation of the rise of Zionism provided by the Syrian *National Socialist Education for the Tenth Grade* textbook refers to an alliance between wealthy Jews and the colonialist nations that created the Zionist movement. That alliance served the interests of both sides, who were looking for new markets for their goods and investments. They decided to take over the entirety of the Arab homeland and convert it to a site where their money could be invested.[10]

The description of Zionism as a product of colonialism is not limited in Syrian textbooks to the period of the creation of the Jewish national movement. The books put a special emphasis on describing the continuous support that they claim the Zionist movement received the continuous support that they claim the Zionist movement received from colonialist powers—especially from Great Britain, until the end of its involvement in the Middle East. Accordingly, a Syrian geography textbook for the fifth grade claims that:

> The British forces left Palestine only after they had helped establish the Zionist entity there. They began by giving the Jews the Balfour declaration (November 2, 1917). They later carried out their promise by facilitating the gradual immigration of hundreds of thousands of Jews to Palestine and allowing them to rob Arab agricultural lands and establish Zionist settlements on them. Due to the crumbling of the Arab countries, the Zionists succeeded, with the cooperation of the imperialist states, to establish in 1948 what they called the state of "Israel" in part of the Arab land of Palestine.[11]

Another textbook asserts that the colonialist support of Zionism reached its peak in November 1947 with the UN vote for the partition of Palestine and the establishment of a Jewish state, "which was passed with the majority of a single vote."[12] Ignoring the fact that Great Britain abstained from the vote, while the Soviet Union and its Eastern bloc allies voted in favor, the Syrian textbooks argue that this was "the worst crime of colonialism"[13] and the "pinnacle of colonialist provocation against the Arab nation."[14] The immediate recognition that Israel received after declaring its independence further revealed the colonialist backing for the Zionist entity.[15] The textbooks also claim that two colonialist states, England and France, supplied Israel with military, financial, and political support. That support reached its peak with the "strategic-colonialist triple alliance against Egypt" during the Sinai Campaign of 1956.[16] Colonialist assistance continued with the increased American aid to Israel, enabling the Zionist state to launch the "aggression of 1967" against the neighboring Arab states.[17] And colonialism helped the Zionist state during the 1973 war, when the United States provided Israel with massive military support. Even in the 1982 Lebanon war, colonialism played its part; according to the Syrian textbook, there existed a "total confluence of colonialist and Zionist interests."[18]

As the preceding demonstrates, Syrian textbooks teach children that the great European colonialist powers were replaced after World War II by the United States, currently the leader of the colonialist power, the United States supports Israel because the latter "serves as a basis for colonialism as its covetous designs are identical to those of colonialism and because it is carrying out the task for which it was created by colonialism."[19] The special relationship between the United States and Israel is described by a fifth-grade textbook in the following way:

> The imperialist states, headed by the U.S., still provide aid of all types to the Israeli gangs which continue to expand and gather the Jews of the world, remove the Arab villages from the lands they occupied, expel their Arab owners, and establish in their place new Zionist settlements.[20]

Zionism is not only an ally of the colonialist powers but, according to the Syrian curriculum, a colonialist movement in and of itself. All definitions of Zionism in Syrian textbooks depict it in that light. A textbook for eighth-grade students, for example, defines Zionism as "a colonialist, racist, aggressive, and expansionist political movement whose goal is to gather all of world Jewry to Palestine."[21] Similarly, in a tenth-grade textbook, Zionism is defined as a racist, colonialist, aggressive, and expansionist movement that is tied to international colonialism. It exploits the Jewish religion to accomplish its goal of establishing a national homeland for the Jews in Palestine and in the neighboring areas.[22] In essence, Syrian textbooks alternate between regarding Zionism as an ally, vanguard, or agent of colonialism. In any case, it is always itself a colonialist movement. If Jewish nationalism is colonialism, then, like all other colonialist powers, it took over a land to which it had no rightful attachment, and thus cannot claim legitimacy in the occupation of Arab land.

Zionism as a Fabrication

The delegitimation campaign leveled at Zionism in Syrian textbooks is not limited to the charge of colonialism. It goes deeper, to the very foundations of Jewish nationalism, and claims that Zionism fabricated not only a national identity but also a connection between it and the land of Israel. That means that the Jewish right to a homeland in Palestine is similar to the British claim to India, or the French claim to Algeria.

According to *National [Pan-Arab] Socialist Education for the Tenth Grade,* Jews fabricated the claim that the Jews of the world are a nation, rather than just a religious sect, and that there is a unique Jewish national identity.[23] By exploiting the Jewish religion, asserts the book, the Zionists were able to forge a Zionist identity and bring about the gathering of the Jewish exiles in Palestine.[24] In reality, however, the Jews of the world "belong to different nations and to many states."[25]

The argument that Zionism is based on a fabrication is explained in greater detail to eighth-grade students. *National [Pan-Arab] Socialist Education for the Eighth Grade* elaborates on what it describes as the "false claims of Zionism."[26] Among the Zionist "lies and false claims" the book lists the following arguments: that the Jews are a single nation sharing a common origin, history, culture, and fate; that Palestine and the surrounding Arab states are the Jewish national homeland; that Jews who live in different areas of the world need to immigrate from their homelands to gather in Palestine; and that Zionism carries an extension of European civilization and development to the Arab East.[27]

The book further offers the students a list of responses or answers to the Zionist "fabrications." Those include the view that Judaism cannot serve as a basis for the formation of a single national identity. Judaism, the book insists, "is a religion followed by many nations, including Falashas from Ethiopia, Tamils from India, Arabs from Yemen, Khazars from Turkey, Slavs, and European Germans."[28] Moreover, claims the book, Palestine could not be the Jewish homeland, because "Arabs resided in it since antiquity."[29] Another argument, having to do with the Zionist call for a gathering of the exiles, claims that "every Jew is a citizen in his country of residence."[30]

After they review those Syrian answers to the Zionist "fabrications," the students are asked to define Zionism and to "list its false claims."[31]

Zionism as Nazism

Syrian children's schoolbooks further invalidate Zionism by comparing it with completely discredited phenomena such as Nazism. The charge that Zionism is Nazism is especially caustic, since Nazi ideology was the most destructive force that Judaism ever faced and is still fresh in the Jewish collective memory. Interestingly, this most devastating of all charges against Zionism receives the highest level of official attention in the textbooks: quotations from President Hafez Al-Assad himself. Thus, Syrian children learn directly from the lion's mouth that Zionism is worse than Nazi ideology.

In his remarks to the Islamic Summit meeting in Kuwait in 1981, as quoted by a textbook for the tenth grade, President Assad drew a comparison between Zionism and Nazism that presents the movements as practically identical, with only minuscule differences between them. Like Nazism, said the Syrian president, Zionism pretends to racial superiority because it views the Jews as God's chosen people. Like the Nazis, the Zionists conquer other nations' lands in the guise of their security concerns, and like them, Zionists persecute the local Arab populations. Moreover, similar to Nazism, Zionism is an expansionist movement that poses a great threat not only to the Arabs but to all Muslim nations—and to the rest of the world. As the Syrian president explained:

> The Zionist Jews do not cease to attack Nazism and exploit its actions in order to justify their own. But what is the difference between the essence of Nazism and Zionism? The Nazis claimed racial superiority and the Zionists claim they are *Allah*'s chosen people, who all other nations must be subjugated to. The Nazis justified their occupation of others' lands and their enslavement by claiming that they needed *lebensraum*. The Zionists occupy other people's lands under the guise of guaranteeing the security borders of the state which they established out of wrongdoing and through aggression against other [people's] lands. The Nazis persecuted and exiled other nations and the Zionists are doing the same today to the Arabs, and will tomorrow do it to the Islamic nations, and the rest of the nations, if an end will not be put to their crimes and to their violations of agreements, norms, and international laws.[32]

Zionism is defined as a Nazi ideology also by the ruling Ba'ath Party. Quoting the fourth part (entitled "General Studies") of the party's indoctrination booklet, a textbook for eighth-grade children describes Zionism as a "racial Nazi movement which strives to settle in the part of the Arab homeland which stretches from the Euphrates to the Nile."[33]

Zionism as Racism

The process of delegitimating the Zionist movement continues in Syrian textbooks with their definition of Zionism as racism. That classification goes beyond the comparison of Zionism to Nazism. Zionism is no longer merely compared with a destructive and racist movement, but rather becomes racism itself.

According to the Syrian textbooks, especially those for high-school students, the founders of Zionism, who were European Jews, held racist attitudes toward the Arabs in Palestine and neighboring countries. The Zionists who came to settle in Palestine, therefore, are not viewed by the Syrian curriculum as members of a fellow Semitic race, but rather as European outsiders and followers of a racist, anti-Semitic ideology. That is part of a larger theme in the textbooks that juxtaposes the Arab conflict with Europe against the Arab conflict with Zionism. In a manner that echoes the United Nations' 1975 "Zionism is racism" resolution, a Syrian history textbook stresses that:

> Zionism is a racist political movement which was established by European Jews during the second half of the nineteenth century. Its goal was to create a national homeland for the Jews, but the Zionists were divided on the issue of [its] location, and eventually decided on Palestine.[34]

Zionism is described by a Syrian reader for the tenth grade as more racist in its treatment of the Palestinians than the North American settlers were toward the Indians, or than the whites in Rhodesia were toward the blacks. The following passage also teaches that there were no real differences of opinion among the various Zionist leaders regarding the treatment of the Palestinian Arabs: even the apparently dissenting voices were in fact as racist as the rest, disagreeing only as to methods. Repeating its claim that Zionism is based on a fabrication, the book explains:

> Zionism views itself as a national ideology which is based on the claim that the Jews are a united people with a unified past, a single general goal and a single fate, despite the fact that it was dispersed [throughout the world] for hundreds of years. From the beginning, Zionism presented itself as an answer to the Jewish question and called upon all Jews in the world to immigrate to the "promised land" in order to re-

new their national lives which were cut off due to the exile. This call was accompanied by a chauvinist attitude that was characterized by discrimination, condescension, and denial of others' rights. Their treatment of the Palestinian Arabs in particular was more racist than that of the Americans toward the Indians or the people of Rhodesia toward the Africans. The views of the leaders of Zionism were unified with regard to the question of ridding themselves of the Arabs, despite the fact that there were sometimes differences of opinion regarding the means that should be used.[35]

The connection between racist Zionist ideology and Nazism is obvious, according to a later passage in this Syrian textbook. As a chauvinistic and aggressive movement, Zionism served as both the predecessor and the inspiration to Nazi ideology. In fact, insists the Syrian author, Zionism was ideologically superior to Nazism, because it represented a clearer and more consistent set of ideas:

> The chauvinist and aggressive-militaristic attitudes are inseparable. They constituted the core of Nazi ideology during the 1930s. People tend to forget that the precedence of this attitude was found in Zionist thinking. It preceded Nazism chronologically, and was superior in terms of clarity [of ideas].[36]

Thus, the process of delegitimating Zionism in the Syrian education system is complete: not only is Zionism an ally of colonialism and a colonialist movement itself, but it is also an ideology based on lies and fabrications that should be compared with Nazism and, transcendently, is the ultimate racist movement that inspired Nazi thought.

Notes

1. *National [Pan-Arab] Socialist Education for the Tenth Grade*, 1998–1999, p. 45.
2. Ibid., p. 100. Similar ideas are presented in other textbooks. See for example, *Modern History of the Arabs for the Ninth Grade, 1999–2000*, p. 127.
3. *National [Pan-Arab] Socialist Education for the Tenth Grade, 1998–1999*, pp. 121–25.
4. Ibid., p. 122.
5. Ibid., p. 121.
6. *National [Pan-Arab] Socialist Education for the Eighth Grade, 1999–2000*, p. 94. Deir Yassin was the site of a mass killing of Palestinian Arab villagers in 1948, and Kfar Kana is the Lebanese village accidentally shelled by Israelis in 1996.

7. Ibid., pp. 122–23.

8. Ibid., p.89.

9. Vladimir Ilich Lenin, *Imperialism, the Highest Stage of Capitalism* (New York: International Publishers, circa 1939).

10. *National [Pan-Arab] Socialist Education for the Tenth Grade, 1998–1999*, p. 89.

11. *The Geography of Syria (Bilad al-Sham) for the Fifth Grade, 1999–2000*, p. 36. *Bilad al-Sham* includes the areas of Syria, Lebanon, Trans-Jordan, and Palestine.

12. *National [Pan-Arab] Socialist Education for the Tenth Grade, 1998–1999*, p. 124.

13. *National [Pan-Arab] Socialist Education for the Eighth Grade, 1999–2000*, p. 87.

14. *National [Pan-Arab] Socialist Education for the Tenth Grade, 1998–1999*, p. 114.

15. Ibid., p.124.

16. Ibid.

17. Ibid.

18. Ibid., p. 125.

19. *National [Pan-Arab] Socialist Education for the Eighth Grade, 1999–2000*, p. 47.

20. *The Geography of Syria (Bilad al-Sham) for the Fifth Grade, 1999–2000*, p. 37.

21. *National [Pan-Arab] Socialist Education for the Eighth Grade, 1999–2000*, p. 92.

22. *National [Pan-Arab] Socialist Education for the Tenth Grade, 1998–1999*, p. 89.

23. Ibid.

24. Ibid.

25. Ibid.

26. *National [Pan-Arab] Socialist Education for the Eighth Grade, 1999–2000*, pp. 93–95.

27. Ibid., pp. 93–94.

28. Ibid., p. 94.

29. Ibid.

30. Ibid.

31. Ibid., p. 95.

32. *National [Pan-Arab] Socialist Education for the Tenth Grade, 1998–1999*, p. 93. Assad's speech to the Islamic Summit in Kuwait was delivered on January 27, 1981.

33. *National [Pan-Arab] Socialist Education for the Eighth Grade, 1999–2000*, p. 96.

34. *Modern History of the Arabs for the Ninth Grade, 1999–2000*, p. 97.

35. *National [Pan-Arab] Socialist Education for the Tenth Grade, 1998–1999*, p. 99.

36. Ibid.

3

Zionism Endangers the Arab World

Syrian textbooks for children in the fourth to eleventh grades depict Zionism as a danger to the Arab world. Zionism endangers Arabs on various levels: the state it created divides the Arab world and prevents its unity; it is the reason for the backwardness of the Arab nations; and it is an aggressive movement that strives to take over the Arab world. Each of those threats necessitates a permanent struggle against Zionism and the Jewish state.

Interestingly, Zionism and Israel are depicted in the Syrian textbooks as omnipotent. Not accurately describing the inequality between Israel and the Arab world in terms of size and population, the Syrian education system portrays Israel as an all-powerful and intimidating enemy. That enemy, according to the textbooks, has the ability to shape the nature and character of Arab societies—perpetuating their backwardness—and to control the relationship between them—perpetuating their divisiveness. The permanent Arab struggle against Israel cannot be abandoned, because it is the Arab world's fight for its ability to determine its own future.

Zionism as a Threat to Arab Nationalism

Possibly the greatest threat that Zionism poses to the Arab world, claim the Syrian textbooks, results from the very presence of a Jewish state in the center of the Arab world: it divides the Arabs and prevents them from uniting. That is a very serious charge, especially if one takes into account Ba'athist ideology, the main goal of which is the creation of a pan-Arab union.

The physical location of Israel—in the heart of the Arab world—disrupts Arab unity. That charge is repeated in textbooks for children of different ages. A fifth-grade geography textbook states that "the Zionist entity concentrates all of its efforts . . . in crumbling the Arab states in order to weaken them."[1] Similarly, a textbook for the tenth grade describes the Zionist movement as a creation of international colonialism meant to "undermine the unity of the Arab states, their development and prosperity."[2] Another textbook, for the eighth grade, quoting a Ba'ath Party's ideological booklet, describes Zionism as a cancer in the heart of the Arab homeland, which prevents its unification:

> This Zionist colonialism . . . is similar to a malignant and lethal cancer which broke out in part of the heart of the Arab homeland—occupied Palestine—and is trying to spread into other parts of the Arab homeland at the expense of the Arab nation as a whole. By so doing, the Zionist colonialist . . . existence in the occupied part of Palestine totally negates the existence of the Arab nation on its land, becoming a stumbling block before the Arab nation [preventing it from] fulfilling its unity and developing its resources.[3]

The same textbook also elaborates on the notion that Israel is the central barrier preventing the unification of the Arab East and West. It further blames Israeli aggression for the failure of all past attempts of the Arabs to unify:

> The establishment of Israel on the land of Palestine constitutes a barrier which separates the East of the Arab homeland from its West and has led to its division, preventing the establishment of Arab unity and sabotaging relations among the Arabs. Any rapprochement between two Arab states leads Israel to threaten and act aggressively against it.[4]

In other words, Israel's very existence challenges the foundations of Arab nationalism and unity. They cannot coexist. Only one can eventually survive, and Arab nationalism must, therefore, prevail over Zionism. That dictates the necessity of a prolonged and eternal Syrian conflict with Israel and Zionism, since a halt in the struggle would mean the collapse of Ba'athist ideology. A compromise would imply that the Syrian state has lost its raison d'être. Therefore, in describing the struggle against Israel, the Syrian textbooks discuss the "annihilation of the Zionist enemy." They quote President Assad on the need to combat Israel, and they speak hopefully of achieving Arab unity at some future date:

> Syria operates in keeping with the revolution of the Arab Socialist Ba'ath party, and under the leadership of the comrade, the man of struggle, Hafez Al-Assad, to mass Arab resources in order to annihilate the Zionist colonialist existence in the Arab land and to liberate all the occupied Arab land. The comrade, the man of struggle, Hafez Al-Assad, expressed this by saying: "In the Arab-Israeli conflict we are struggling against the world Zionist movement. This is the racist, expansionist, and aggressive movement that gave birth to a colonialist invasion carried out by Israel with unlimited support by the colonialist forces."[5]

Zionism as Responsible for the Backwardness of the Arab World

According to the Syrian textbooks, Zionism also damages the Arab nation by preventing it from modernizing. That is because the establishment of Israel confronted Arabs with a situation of prolonged military conflict, diverting all Arab resources to the war effort. Such forced backwardness benefits the colonialists, who can easily maintain their control of the underdeveloped Arab world. But that burden, according to Syrian schoolbooks, does not mean that the Arab world will abandon the struggle against Zionism in order to modernize. Indeed, backwardness is a price the Arab world gladly pays to rid itself of its greatest enemy, Zionism. As a textbook for the eighth grade stresses,

> The existence of Israel at the heart of the Arab homeland created a condition of permanent tension in the region and pushed the Arabs to allocate much of their resources to the war effort. This slows down the development and industrialization works . . . and leads to a backwardness which makes it easier for colonialism to maintain its control and

exploitation. But the Arabs . . . are willing to use all their resources in order to rid themselves of the danger that threatens their existence.[6]

Once again, the image of Israel that emerges is that of an ultimate danger to the Arab people. Hence, not even the underdevelopment conceded by the textbooks would lead them to compromise with Israel; the notion is rejected out of hand. The nature of the Zionist threat, Syrian children learn, is so dangerous to Arabs that they must be forever entangled in a zero-sum conflict against Israel. Arabs everywhere must accept their economic and social realities unquestioningly and be ready to make the necessary sacrifices in order to keep Arab society mobilized against the Zionist danger.

Zionism as an Aggressive, Expansionist Movement

Zionism and the state of Israel pose a great physical threat to the Arab world, insist the Syrian textbooks. As an expansionist movement by definition, Zionism must gain control of the land and economic resources of the Arab world, which would serve as a homeland to all of world Jewry. Moreover, the books claim that Israel's military forces do not serve a defensive function, but rather an aggressive one, and that Israel's concept of "secure borders" is a sham that hides its true aggressive nature.

The notion that Zionism is an aggressive and expansionist movement is present in textbooks for children of all ages, but the presentation of this theme becomes more elaborate from one grade to the next. Small children learn it through stories that teach about Israel's use of military force for expansionist purposes. On all levels, the underlying conclusion is that the Syrian people, and indeed Arabs as a whole, must never abandon the struggle against the Zionist enemy's attempts to gain control of the whole Arab world.

A fifth-grade textbook illustrates this theme with the story of a little Syrian girl's dream. Layla dreams that Zionist soldiers come into her house and expel her and her family. The lesson of the story is that the Israeli state expelled the Palestinian Arabs from their homeland, and that the Syrian people must struggle both to redress that wrong and to avoid a similar fate themselves. The story also serves to indoctrinate children into the ideology of Arab unity: they are taught that the people of Syria must combat Israel on behalf of their suffering Palestinian brothers. It reads like this:

> [In her dream Layla] heard voices of people entering the courtyard of her home. . . . In the darkness she saw armed people expelling her father and mother from the house. Layla told herself: "These are surely thieves." Within several moments they entered her room and told her in a dry tone: "Go ahead. Get out of the house."
>
> She told them: "But this is our house. Why are you expelling us from it?"
>
> They said: "Get out without arguing. Get out quickly, otherwise we will kill you."
>
> They held her by the hand and dragged her violently. They had many weapons and their faces were angry like the face of Satan. They threw Layla in the street and she screamed: "This is an injustice, this is occupation, this is plundering. You are throwing us out of our home. Where will we live?"
>
> They answered: "Go to the desert and live there in a tent. Go to hell."
>
> [Layla wakes up and discusses the dream with her father.]
>
> Her father told her: "This is what actually took place in Palestine, but it happened, my daughter, in reality and not in a dream. Our land was invaded by foreigners who came from faraway lands carrying many weapons. They expelled the people from their homes and settled in them as occupiers and robbers."
>
> Layla said: "But this is an occupation and an aggression. We must not remain silent about this injustice. We must fight against these aggressors until we gain back our homeland, Father."
>
> Said the father: "Correct, my daughter. We fight against those Zionist aggressors and will not remain silent until we restore Palestine to its owners "[7]

After reading the story the children are asked: "What did Layla feel when she screamed? Who were the aggressive strangers? Was what she saw a dream or a reality?"[8] Students are led to conclude that Layla's dream was the reality of the Zionist takeover of Palestine, and that aggression could face Arabs everywhere. The story mobilizes children to participate in the struggle against Israel, the Satan-like enemy that has been so merciless in its treatment of Arabs.

A Syrian textbook for the sixth grade strengthens the conclusions of the fifth-grade text. When learning about "Palestine," the children are told that "the covetous aspirations of the Zionist enemy in Palestine and in the Arab land know no limits and one can not predict how far these aspirations will go. The Zionists are not thinking of returning the stolen land to its owners."[9] That Israel moved toward resolving the conflict with the Palestinians by signing the Oslo accords in 1993—and by withdrawing since then from the most populated portion of the West Bank—is not reflected in this or any other Syrian textbook. All these books, however, published after 1997—at least four years after the signing and after the PLO's entry into the territories—do refer to other recent events.

Zionism's aggression is also stressed in a book for the tenth grade. That aggression, insists the text, is expressed in the belief that the use of brute force is the best means to achieve political goals.[10] The book asserts that Israel's military force is not defensive and that the Zionist aggression did not result from a preceding Arab aggression or from a defensive need, as the Israelis often like to claim. Rather, Israel's military force is aggressive in orientation, and its operational goals are "openly expansionist."[11] The book alleges that over the years, Israel's expansionist ambitions were guided by a "plan of stages" aimed at creating a "greater Israel"[12]; that having taken over the land of Palestine, Israel is now "trying to spread and expand like a cancer on the other parts of the Arab homeland."[13] The Syrian education system explains the aggressive-militant Israeli attitude in psychological terms as a response to a "repressed inner need."[14]

In the eighth grade, students become familiar with the full details of the Israeli plan to take over the Arab lands in stages. The first stage is an Israeli annexation of the Sinai Peninsula, the East and West Banks of the Jordan River, and some neighboring areas in Syria and Lebanon.[15] The second stage includes "reaching the Euphrates and the Nile."[16] Despite the fact that the book was published in 1999, there is no mention of Israel's withdrawal, in the framework of a peace agreement with Egypt, from the entire Sinai Peninsula more than a decade and a half ago. To portray Israel as the most dangerous and threatening adversary of Syria and the Arab world, history stands still and time is frozen. Education and truth are sacrificed at the altar of the state and its ideology.

The Syrian education system teaches children to view Israel as a demonic threat not only to keep society mobilized, but also to excuse the failures of the Syrian regime. The Ba'ath Party's failure to bring about Arab unity, for example, can simply be blamed on Israel's forceful physical division of the Arab world. Likewise, Syria's dismal economic failure is explained as resulting from the unavoidable battle against Zionism. By teaching children that Israel is an ever-present, colossal threat, the Syrian regime tries to distract its youth from questioning its grim performance or rebelling against their bleak living conditions and limited opportunities.

Notes

1. *The Geography of Syria (Bilad al-Sham) for the Fifth Grade, 1999–2000*, p. 38.
2. *National [Pan-Arab] Socialist Education for the Tenth Grade, 1998–1999*, p. 60.
3. *National [Pan-Arab] Socialist Education for the Eighth Grade, 1999–2000*, p. 96.
4. Ibid., pp. 47–48.
5. Ibid., p. 48.
6. Ibid.
7. *Reader for the Fifth Grade, 1998–1999, Part II*, pp. 43–45.
8. Ibid., p. 46.
9. *Reader for the Sixth Grade, 1997–1998, Part II*, p. 95.
10. *National [Pan-Arab] Socialist Education for the Tenth Grade, 1998–1999*, p. 96.
11. Ibid.
12. Ibid., p. 114.
13. Ibid., p. 112.
14. Ibid., p. 114.
15. *National [Pan-Arab] Socialist Education for the Eighth Grade, 1999–2000*, pp. 45–46.
16. Ibid.

4

The Arab-Israeli Conflict

The history of the Arab-Israeli conflict plays a central role in Syrian textbooks. Syrian children are taught about the various Arab-Israeli wars, and they learn that the conflict with Israel and Zionism is a prolonged affair during which the Arab armies have continuously attempted to liberate occupied Palestine. The children also learn that their conflict with Israel stands at the core of their self-definition as Syrian citizens and Arab nationalists. That concept is reflected in a textbook for the tenth grade that defines one of the central goals of the Arab national movement after World War II as the "struggle against the Zionist covetous aspirations in Palestine and in the Arab homeland."[1] Thus Syrian children are raised to be members of the Arab nationalist movement, and they internalize the message that they must participate in the fight against Zionism. The ideas of citizenship and identity are interlocked with the concept of the struggle against Israel.

Among the various conflicts with Israel, the Syrian education system pays particular attention to the 1948 war, which it describes as a devastating Arab defeat, and to the 1973 war, which it calls the "liberating *Tishrin* war."[2] (*Tishrin,* corresponding to October, is the month on the Muslim calendar during which the war erupted.) But even the glorious victory of 1973 "is not the end of the conflict between the Arabs and racist Zionism."[3] That conflict is prolonged, difficult, and may require the citizens of the Syrian state to make many sacrifices;

24

but it is not hopeless. It will continue "until the occupied Arab land is liberated in full and the Zionist colonialist settlement in the Arab land will cease to exist."[4] Eventual victory is assured, and the conflict will cease after the Arabs deal Zionism a fatal blow.

In the textbooks, discussion of victory against Israel is tied to a condition of Arab unity. Lack of unity is said to be one of the root causes for the repeated failures of the Arab states to defeat Israel. Other causes, according to a ninth-grade textbook, include the betrayal of some Arab leaders, the inferior weaponry of the Arab armies, and the "imperialist support of Israel."[5]

The influence of those factors, claims a history textbook for the ninth grade, was particularly evident in the results of the war of 1948. After the British left Palestine, it explains, terrorist Jewish groups, armed with weapons given to them by the British before they left the country, began attacking Arab villages and committing atrocities— for example, in Deir Yassin.[6] Discussing those events, the book omits any mention of the increased tensions between Arabs and Jews in Palestine, which were already high during the period of the British mandate. The Arabs are portrayed solely as the victims of those unprovoked Zionist attacks, whose aim was "to threaten the Arabs and to force them to leave their homes."[7] In response to those Jewish actions, Arabs in all the neighboring countries formed an army and attacked Israel. Initially, continues the history book, the Arab forces were successful, but Israel was saved by the United States and England, which forced the Arabs to cease fire in June 1948. That changed the tide, because the Zionists "used the cease-fire to acquire advanced weapons and airplanes . . . while the Arabs remained in their previous condition."[8] The result was a great Arab defeat, given the Arab term *Nakbah,* "the disaster," in Syrian textbooks.

The textbooks describe the results of the *Nakbah* of 1948 as devastating for the Arabs. A tenth-grade text lists its consequences as including, among other woes, the establishment of Israel as an aggressive colonialist base for struggle against the Arab nation; the exile of more than 750,000 Palestinians from their homeland to the neighboring countries; the forced submission of more than 180,000 Arabs to the "oppressive Israeli regime"; the Israeli annexation of the West Bank from Jordan, and the Gaza Strip from Egypt; and the removal of the name "Palestine" from the world atlas.[9]

But the defeat of 1948 also influenced inter-Arab relations and the degree of unity achieved by the Arab world. The more interesting part of the list deals with those consequences of the war that directly influenced the Ba'athist regime in Syria. Among those, *National [Pan-Arab] Socialist Education for the Tenth Grade* lists "the unmasking of some Arab regimes that were connected to colonialism" as one of the most important. Although it glorifies Arab unity, the revolutionary regime in Syria does not hesitate to teach children to distinguish between the friends and foes of Ba'athism in the Arab world.[10]

Other consequences of the war, which relate to the revolutionary nature of Ba'athist ideology, are said to include "forcing the Arab public to face the need to have an all-inclusive Arab revolution."[11] The revolutionary tone does not end here, and among the positive outcomes of the *Nakbah* the book also includes "paving the way for an increased role of the revolutionary movement and its struggle to establish progressive regimes."[12] The Syrian regime, therefore, still views the Arab defeat of 1948 as having created unique opportunities for spreading its revolutionary message and further radicalizing the Arab world.

If 1948 was a defeat, then 1973 is portrayed as its complete antithesis. The difference is important. If the *Nakbah* of the 1948 war indicted the old Arab elite as colonialist stooges, then the war launched by Ba'athism must be portrayed as a vindication of the new elite. Thus the 1973 war, claims a textbook for the eighth grade, "lifted high the heads of the Arabs, returned confidence to the human and the Arab soldier's soul, and proved to the whole world the Arab nation's ability to stand firm and struggle for the liberation of its land and the expulsion of the plundering occupier."[13]

The war, according to a textbook for the ninth grade, was only another stage in the Arab struggle against international imperialism and its step-daughter, Israel.[14] It resulted from a combination of factors, including Israeli aspirations to expand and occupy more Arab lands; Arab disillusionment with Israel, which continued to ignore UN resolutions calling on it to withdraw from the territories it had conquered in 1967; a growing opposition to Israel among Palestinians; and an Arab need to avenge their defeats in previous wars.[15]

The war of 1973, which the Syrian textbooks portray as such an awesome victory, did not end with the annihilation of Israel, defined by Syrian ideology as a necessary precondition for achieving Arab unity. Explaining that shortcoming, the Syrian textbooks throw blame on Syria's principal partner in the war, Egypt. The war, they explain, failed on the Egyptian front, which delayed the Arab forces' advancement. Later, a UN-sponsored cease-fire was unavoidable, despite very impressive Syrian accomplishments on Israel's northern front.[16]

Ba'athism and the Palestinian Question

The discussion of the Palestinian question in Syrian textbooks addresses the state's deep commitment to the concept of Arab unity. The Palestinians and their struggle for statehood are described with a great deal of empathy. Stories about Palestinians who fought against Israel are presented in a heroic manner, emphasizing the need for Syrian children to emulate such acts of sacrifice for the Arab homeland. The textbooks portray Israel as engaged in heinous acts of oppression toward the Palestinians.

The Palestinian issue, however, is not discussed for its own merit. Rather, the textbooks present it as the pivot of the broader conflict between the Arab nation and Zionism. The issue therefore assumes central significance as an example and proof of the regime's support for Arab unity. That aspect of pan-Arab nationalism reveals the emphasis placed by the Syrian state on instilling its own ideology in its youngsters' minds.

Reflecting the regime's outlook, Syrian textbooks delineate Palestine as the very center of the Arab world, describing its geographical location as "similar to that of the heart in the body."[17] That heart, according to Syrian ideology, is under pressure because of the existence of Israel. The problem is even greater because Israel is also the factor that divides the Arab world in half and prevents it from unifying. The Palestinian problem and the issue of Arab unity are, therefore, inseparable. For the dream of unity to be fulfilled, the Palestinian question must be resolved by the destruction of the Israeli state.

Syrian students are taught the importance of the Palestinian problem at least as early as the fifth grade. A geography textbook's portrayal of the Palestinians as innocent victims of Israeli brutality is pitched to evoke emotions in children and create feelings of empathy toward their Palestinian brothers. A picture showing the expulsion of the

Palestinians by the Israeli military accompanies a text that describes the establishment of Israel in 1948: "They [the Israelis] committed atrocities against the Arabs which forced them to abandon their land in Palestine and find refuge in neighboring Arab countries."[18]

That Israeli cruelty, according to a book entitled *Reader for the Sixth Grade,* created a moral dilemma for many people, who called on Israel to return the Palestinians to their homes and give them national rights. Only the support that Israel receives from "the imperialist powers" saved it from having to solve the problem.[19] Four years later, in the tenth grade, Israel's treatment of the Palestinians is described in even darker terms; it was not only an expulsion, but an attempt to annihilate the Palestinian people.[20]

In stark contrast to their description of Israel, the Syrian textbooks portray the Palestinian struggle for independence in heroic terms. Palestinians who fought against Israel are not merely brave, but national idols whose actions must be emulated. The Palestinian struggle against Israel not only is completely justified, but is also a struggle for individual and national honor.[21] Palestinian heroism is celebrated in a sixth-grade textbook that proclaims, "Our Palestinian brothers sacrificed their blood until the world heard their voice and recognized their problem. They continue to die in the field of honor, but only after they inflict, in defense of their land, heavy losses of life and property on the enemy."[22] A ninth-grade textbook describes the Palestinian struggle for independence in similar terms. After briefly reviewing the history of the Palestinian national movement, the book states that "the Palestinian Arab people still fight through all means and make sacrifices in order to regain their full rights."[23]

The Palestinian issue is not only a matter of emotions, however. It also concerns high politics bearing on inter-Arab relations. A ninth-grade textbook presents in full the formal position of the Ba'ath Party toward the Palestinian problem, "the foremost problem of the Arabs." The Ba'ath completely "support the Palestinian revolution" and the Palestinian people's "return to their homeland and their self-determination on their land." The party calls for unity among the various Palestinian resistance factions and, again, describes the adversary of Palestinian nationalism—Zionism—as a "racist, aggressive, expansionist movement, which has clear ties to imperialism."[24]

The Palestinian issue is central to the development of Syrian/pan-Arab identity, and the textbooks stress that the "fighter comrade" Hafez Al-Assad completely supports the Palestinian cause. Syrian children learn that under his leadership, Syria offered military, political, and material assistance to the Palestinians. That assistance culminated in 1973, when Assad led a war against Israel, one goal of which was "the liberation of *all* the occupied land"[25]—not merely the Golan Heights, which Israel conquered directly from Syria, but also the West Bank and the Gaza Strip, considered to be occupied "Arab lands" belonging to the Palestinians. The students further learn that President Assad initiated a political campaign during the 1973 Arab Summit in Algeria, in an attempt to create a unified Arab plan of action regarding the Palestinian issue. That plan called for two stages. The first was the complete liberation of all Arab lands occupied by Israel in 1967. The second had to do with the territory of Israel proper and called for protecting "Arab sovereignty in Jerusalem."[26] The text makes no distinction between the East and the West parts of the city.

The description in the ninth grade textbook of Syria's position, both in the 1973 war and during the Arab Summit in Algeria, reveals the regime's political agenda. In both cases, Syria portrays itself as the key defender among Arab states of the Palestinian cause. Beyond demonstrating its commitment to the cause of Arab unity, Syria assumes the mantle of its leadership. In describing itself as the chief patron of the Palestinians, Syria lays claim to being the leading force on the most central Arab issue.[27]

Notes

1. *National [Pan-Arab] Socialist Education for the Tenth Grade, 1998–1999*, p. 63.
2. *National [Pan-Arab] Socialist Education for the Eighth Grade, 1999–2000*, p. 97.
3. Ibid.
4. Ibid.
5. *National [Pan-Arab] Socialist Education for the Ninth Grade*, p. 71.
6. *Modern History of the Arabs for the Ninth Grade, 1999–2000*, p. 172.
7. Ibid.
8. Ibid., p. 173.
9. *National [Pan-Arab] Socialist Education for the Tenth Grade, 1998–1999*, pp.134–35.

10. This passage relates directly to a broader theme found in many Ba'athist documents. For example, the following is a communique from the Ba'ath Party Organization Bureau in Syria: "The enemies of the people realized that armed conspiracy would only make the Party stronger and more determined. . . . Therefore, the imperialist media and Arab reactionaries . . . exploited sectarianism, regionalism and tribalism as a means to bring an end to the Party. . . . The pollution was thus able to seep through into the minds of some people and undermine the ideals of many to such an extent that they felt no shame or hesitation in dealing with the Party's affairs on a sectarian or regional basis. They thus strayed into the treacherous quagmire of deviation and became, whether they knew it or not, a tool for the fifth column. . . . Such a person should be punished as though he were an enemy of the people." A full text of the communique can be found in Nikolas Van Dam, *The Struggle for Power in Syria: Politics and Society under Assad and the Ba'ath Party* (New York: I.B. Tauris Publishers, 1996), pp. 146–51.

11. *National [Pan-Arab] Socialist Education for the Tenth Grade, 1998–1999*, p. 135.

12. Ibid.

13. *National [Pan-Arab] Socialist Education for the Eighth Grade, 1999–2000*, p. 97.

14. *Modern History of the Arabs for the Ninth Grade, 1999–2000*, p. 159.

15. Ibid.

16. Ibid.

17. *Reader for the Sixth Grade, Part II, 1997–1998*, p. 94.

18. *The Geography of Syria (Bilad al-Sham) for the Fifth Grade, 1999–2000*, p. 36.

19. *Reader for the Sixth Grade, Part II, 1997–1998*, pp. 94–95.

20. *National [Pan-Arab] Socialist Education for the Tenth Grade, 1998–1999*, p. 60.

21. It is interesting to note the degree to which the distinction between the public and the private realms is blurred in the textbooks. In the discussion of the Palestinian struggle, for example, there is no distinction between personal and national honor.

22. *Reader for the Sixth Grade, Part II, 1997–1998*, p. 95.

23. *National [Pan-Arab] Socialist Education for the Ninth Grade*, p. 70.

24. Ibid., p. 73.

25. Ibid., pp. 73–74, emphasis mine.

26. Ibid. p. 74.

27. This Syrian position, rooted in the Ba'ath ideology—which perceives Syria as "the heart of Arabism"—on the one hand, and Palestinian aspirations for political particularism within the Arab world on the other, have brought Syria and the Palestinians into political conflict and even occasional military clashes, particularly in Lebanon over the past three decades.

5

The Struggle against Israel and the Peace Process

As noted, Syrian textbooks frequently discuss the struggle against Israel. They describe the conflict as permanent and unresolvable as long as Israel continues to exist. Moreover, the nature of the conflict necessitates that even children be educated to sacrifice their lives and wage *Jihad* [Holy War] against Israel. In some of the books' more chilling passages, Syrian children are exhorted to die at the altar of that struggle. They are told that such an act is their religious and national duty and that they will be rewarded for it both in this world—by the state, which will honor them and their families—and in the Hereafter, by *Allah*.

In this context, naturally, there is no room for education toward peace or normalized relations with Israel. The fact that Israel and Syria have engaged in some form of negotiations since 1991 is not even mentioned in these textbooks. Instead, children are taught that making peace with Israel is a betrayal of Arab causes. But the textbooks do not simply avoid teaching children about the possibility of peace. Rather, their lessons teach children to be ready to participate in the battle against the Zionist enemy at any time, in effect serving to mobilize young Syrians to war.

The Struggle against Israel

As the Syrian textbooks demonstrate, Ba'athist ideology demands an inexorable and ceaseless conflict with Israel. The Syrian government, whose reign is based on Ba'athism, cannot reconcile the contradiction between that ideology and peaceful relations with Israel. Since the party that rules the Syrian state is so fixated on the cause of Arab unity and views Israel as the main obstacle for achieving that goal, peace with the Zionist state would undermine the fundamental tenets of the regime.

A textbook for the fifth grade explains to students that the Arab people continuously struggle against the Zionist occupation "in all means available, including an armed struggle."[1] Here, the Syrian curriculum speaks of the armed struggle against Israel as an ongoing and ever-lasting reality. Similarly, an eighth-grade book teaches Syrian children that the wars Syria fought against Israel did not bring an end to the conflict with Zionism. After praising the Syrian achievements in the 1973 war, the textbook states:

> This war is not the end of the Arab conflict with racist Zionism. It is but a chapter in a series of wars of liberation . . . until the occupied land is fully liberated and the Zionist colonialist settlement in the Arab land ends.[2]

One of the problems for the state is, how does the Syrian curriculum deal with the fact that the Israeli state remained invincible, despite the various Arab-Israeli wars? How can it continue to instill Syrian children with enough confidence and hope to expect an eventual Arab victory? The curriculum's response to that problem is to make historic analogies to the Crusaders and Tartars who conquered the Middle East. Like those conquerors, Israel is portrayed as a fundamentally alien presence in the region. As the Arab-Islamic forces defeated the alien Christian Crusaders, assert the textbooks, the foreign Jewish/Zionist presence in the Middle East will be removed by the Arabs, even if the battle is prolonged and lasts for many years.

Zionism is compared with the Crusaders beginning in the fifth grade. Here the students learn about the battle of Hittin, which took place in the Galilee in 1187.[3] There Arab and Crusader forces fought for control of the region. After learning that the Crusaders initiated the fight without any provocation, the students read about the great battle during which the Arab forces of Salah Al-Din [Saladin] clashed with the Christian forces under the command of Richard the Lion Hearted.[4] The Arab victory in Hittin is celebrated in the textbook as an act that "stopped the Crusaders' aggressiveness and purified Arab land from aggressors."[5] The lessons of the story are made clear by a question that follows the text. The assignment asks the children, "How will we purify our Arab land in Palestine and liberate it from the Zionist aggressors?"[6]

Similarly, a textbook for the sixth grade compares the establishment of the state of Israel with the occupation of the country by the Tartars and Crusaders. Those alien powers were eventually defeated by Arab forces. Israel will face a similar fate. The analogy instills in the children the importance of unity in the Arab rank and file:

> The Arabs must return to their ancient history and learn a lesson from it. When the Tartars attacked the Arabs they were unable to overpower them until they unified and consolidated their ranks. When the Crusaders attacked the Arabs, they were unable to defeat them. . . . In this century, as in previous ones, only power helps and only the struggle returns the stolen right.[7]

That text reveals more than just the Syrian regime's attitude toward Israel. It provides a window into the broader values and worldview the Syrian state chooses to instill in the minds of its youth. It shows that Syria educates children to believe that the state of nature—namely, the natural condition of the world—is one in which *homo homini Lupus* [man to man is a wolf]. In that Hobbesian world, it is a war of all against all; everything is determined by power-relations and conflict. Thus, peace with Israel is undesirable at best, unnatural and impossible at worst.

Attitude toward the Peace Process

As was discussed above, the Syrian textbooks generally ignore the peace process between Israel and its Arab neighbors. They include no mention of the Oslo process, the Israeli-Jordanian peace, or the peace negotiations with Syria that began in 1991. The only peace agreement discussed by the textbooks—that between Israel and Egypt—receives marginal attention and is described in wholly negative terms.

A sixth-grade textbook reflects the regime's rejection of the Camp David accords and its view of Egypt as traitor to the Arab cause because it signed a peace agreement with Israel. The text, entitled "The Path of Martyrdom," praises the Arab *Shahids* (martyrs) who died in Lebanon. It describes those Arab leaders willing to make peace with Israel as the internal enemies of the Arab cause. Since such leaders are traitors who put their personal interests before those of their people and, therefore, created divisiveness among the Arab nation, they must be severely punished by the Arab public:

> Oh martyrs . . . you taught [the Israelis] that the defeatist Arab politicians who have defeated souls do not represent the Arab public. You taught them that those who negotiate with them and bow their heads in front of the Israeli executioner do so out of fear for their jobs, their privileges and their money—which they stole from the sweat and blood of the people. You taught them that these are but spies in our midst and traitors of our public. And we will repay them with a harshness that is not less severe than our ruthlessness toward the invaders, but in somewhat different ways that are fit for the agents of the enemy [who are present within] our people. . . . You taught them that the path of Camp David, and other similar paths, are the paths of traitorous death for those who aspire toward and walk them.[8]

The text quoted above reveals not only the Syrian rejection of the Camp David agreements but also the regime's view that Egyptian president Anwar Al-Sadat's assassination by Muslim fundamentalists (who opposed the peace with Israel) was both necessary and justified. All Arab leaders who make peace with Israel are described as traitors upon whom vengeance must be taken.

Moreover, the text portrays peace as a personal whim of certain Arab leaders motivated by personal interests. In so doing, the book creates a dichotomy between the Arab leaders and the Arab public—which, purportedly, always opposes such a move. The tension exists on both ideological and moral levels: unlike their greedy leaders, whose ideological commitment to Arab causes is secondary to their aspirations for personal gain, the Arab public is depicted as impoverished, honest, and fully committed ideologically. Honesty and morality are thus directly opposed to peace with Israel.

In accordance with its opposition to peace, the Syrian regime takes special pride in its role as a leader of the Arab front formed against Egypt after the signing of the Camp David accords. A history book for the ninth grade mentions the accords and states that "[Syria] participated in the establishment of a steadfast resistance front following President Sadat's visit to Jerusalem."[9]

The peace process is also discussed in a textbook for the eighth grade. Here the focus shifts from the Arab leaders to deceptive Israel, which misleads international public opinion by claiming to desire peace. But what it really wants is a narrowly interpreted peace without obligation to fulfill international agreements—effectively, an Arab surrender.[10] The textbook quotes President Assad's observations about the insincere nature of Israel's engagement in the peace process: "Israel, despite its claims that it wants peace, acts, in fact, in the opposite manner."[11]

Despite the criticisms they level at Israel's peace approach and at the Arab leaders who made peace with Israel, the Syrian textbooks are not opposed to the idea of peace. But the manifestation they call for matches the ideology and values of the Ba'ath Party. As *Social Education for the Fifth Grade* rhapsodizes: "This is our way—we the Arabs—to live in peace under the banner of unity, liberty, and socialism, without feeling hatred or resentment toward the people of the world, but treating them with appreciation and love."[12] But in order for this peace to come, "every citizen must defend the homeland, liberate the parts of the Arab land that were stolen, and struggle against Zionism and colonialism."[13] A Syrian peace, in other words, requires Arab unity and the destruction of Zionism and Israel.

Since the Syrian curriculum makes almost no mention of the peace process, viewing it as an act of betrayal, it is not portrayed as an acceptable vehicle for the solution of the Arab-Israeli conflict. The solution proposed by the Syrian education system is "a purification of our Arab land in Palestine and its liberation from the aggressive Zionists."[14] As a father explains to his son in a fourth-grade textbook: "We must liberate Palestine from the Zionists, and return to our beloved city, Acre."[15]

As the cited texts reveal, the Syrian rejection of the peace process is not a dismissal of peace itself but a definition of it in Ba'athist ideological terms, with the precondition of Israel's destruction.

Notes

1. *The Geography of Syria (Bilad al-Sham) for the Fifth Grade, 1999–2000*, p. 38.
2. *National [Pan-Arab] Socialist Education for the Eighth Grade, 1999–2000*, p. 97.
3. *Reader for the Fifth Grade, Part II, 1998–1999*, p. 6.
4. Ibid., p, 8.
5. Ibid.
6. Ibid., p. 9.
7. *Reader for the Sixth Grade, Part II, 1997–1998*, pp. 95–96.
8. *Social [Pan-Arab] Education for the Sixth Grade, 1998–1999*, p. 121.
9. *Modern History of the Arabs for the Ninth Grade, 1999–2000*, p. 160.
10. *National [Pan-Arab] Socialist Education for the Eighth Grade, 1999–2000*, p. 107.
11. Ibid.
12. *Social Education for the Fifth Grade*, p. 97.
13. Ibid.
14. *Reader for the Fifth Grade, Part II, 1998–1999*, p. 9.
15. *Reader for the Fourth Grade, Part I, 1999–2000*, p. 64. The city of Acre is located on the northern part of Israel's Mediterranean coast.

6

Education for Jihad *and Martyrdom*

Syrian textbooks do not merely fail to educate children for peace; they indoctrinate them with the idea that it is their duty to wage *Jihad* [Holy War] and become martyrs in the service of the state and its ideology. *Jihad* is a religious principle. Mainstream Islamic orthodoxy, however, does not regard it as one of the five Pillars of Faith—namely, reciting the *Shahadah* ("There is no God but *Allah,* and Muhammad is his messenger"); fasting during the month of Ramadan; making the pilgrimage to Mecca; prayer; and charity. Only contemporary Islamic fundamentalist movements have turned *Jihad,* in both their writings and actions, into a core tenet of the Islamic faith. The Syrian school system inclines toward the extreme fundamentalist point of view, presenting *Jihad* as a sacred principle to be followed as a personal duty by the students.[1]

That endorsement of a fundamentalist religious doctrine by the Syrian education system is curious, considering Ba'athist ideology's secular origin and its concern with Arab rather than strictly Muslim unification. Secularism, a component of the Ba'ath's socialist pan-Arabism, provided a common denominator to eclipse sectarian divisions not only in Syria and Lebanon but throughout the Arab world. Nevertheless, following Assad's rise to power, the Syrian regime gradually adopted the principles of the "Muslim state," encompassing religious tenets into Ba'athist ideology. That became particularly true after the 1982 clashes with the fundamentalist Muslim Brotherhood, during which the city of Hamma was bombarded to the point of destruction by the regime. About 20,000 of its citizens lost their lives.

The main characteristics of a "Muslim state" were mostly repressive. While permitting Islamic activities, the state enforced full government control through both its security organs and its Ministry of *Awqaf* [religious endowments], which rewarded Islamic groups for loyalty to the state. The school system went above and beyond that "Muslim state" policy by recruiting and utilizing Islamic principles—primarily *Jihad*—in the service of the struggle against Israel.

The Spiritual Aspect

Education for *Jihad* is a central theme in the Syrian textbooks, from the early years of primary school through the last years of high school. Those books, especially the ones relating to the subject of Islamic education, focus on the profitability of martyrdom and its superiority over life. To encourage children to wage *Jihad* against the enemies of the Arabs (primarily Israel),[2] the textbooks threaten that *Allah* punishes those who refuse to die for his sake. They also emphasize stories describing the heroism of both adults and youths who commit martyrdom.

Many of the books deal extensively with the meaning of *Jihad* and the anticipated rewards that both *Allah* and the Syrian state grant those who wage it. *Jihad*, fourth-grade Syrian children are taught, is a "deal" in which the believer sells his soul to *Allah*. In return, he is granted life in Paradise. As *Islamic Education for the Fourth Grade* teaches:

> The believers, the *Jihad* warriors, sold their souls to *Allah* . . . . They defended their faith and their homeland with force and courage and killed many enemies. They were killed for the cause of *Allah* and became eternal martyrs. Therefore, they are worthy of *Allah*'s Paradise . . . . *Allah* had promised them a very large reward . . . . Indeed, *Allah* does not break his promise. *Allah* brings this news to the courageous *Jihad* warriors in order to calm their hearts [so that they would] go fearlessly and enthusiastically to battle . . . . [T]hey are determined to achieve one of two worthy things: victory or martyrdom.[3]

The "deal" in which the believer commits martyrdom offers clear gain. The same textbook even describes martyrdom as a "profitable deal." The believer sells his soul to *Allah* for a high price: a guaranteed passage to Paradise, and many additional benefits. The use of a commercial motif—a business deal—and the emphasis on the benefits given to the one who dies as a martyr are not perceived as improper, despite the fact that the issues discussed are of the highest spiritual nature.

The concept of the "economic" profitability of martyrdom in the Syrian curriculum derives from a well-known Koranic verse that describes it in those terms. The fourth-grade textbook quotes the verse:

> *Allah* has bought from the believers their souls and their properties for they shall inherit Paradise, they will fight for the cause of *Allah* and they will kill [the enemies] and will be killed. This is a promise *Allah* took upon Himself in the Torah, the New Testament, and *The Koran* . . . . Rejoice in the deal you made with Him.[4]

The use of an economic analogy is meant to assist children psychologically in dealing with the issue of their own death. The promised benefits and the businesslike description of the process of martyrdom turns the act, in children's minds, from an irrational and frightening decision to march toward one's own death into an apparently calculated, rational, and even desirable choice. The quotation from *The Koran* even encourages children—as believers—to rejoice in their expected death as a fair price to pay for all the benefits that *Allah* will bestow upon them. To ensure that children grasp the profitability of the deal, they are instructed to answer the following question: "What is the price *Allah* paid for the believers' souls and properties?" And further, "The sale of the believers' souls and properties is a profitable commercial deal and great news. Write down the part of the verse that refers to it."[5]

The Syrian textbooks use intense repetition to imbue in children a preference for death over life. Again and again, young Syrian children are taught to look forward to the promised rewards of the afterlife following their martyrdom. Repetition also helps to overcome the initial objection felt to voluntary death. For that reason, *Islamic Education for the Fourth Grade* states again, in another context, that "the belief in *Allah* and in his Messenger [the Prophet Muhammad] and in the *Jihad* by sacrificing the soul, is a commercial deal introducing those who accomplish it to Paradise."[6] After reading that text, the children are asked again, "What is the reward of the *Jihad* warriors [who die] for the cause of *Allah*?"[7]

Since the "profitable deal" is voluntary, Syrian students must learn to desire it and, by extension, their own deaths. Therefore, after having learned about it in the fourth grade, students in the fifth grade are encouraged to enter such a deal when they read that for Muslim believers, death is preferable to life. *Allah*'s reward to the *Jihad* warriors is so great, it "makes the believers see death for the cause of *Allah* favorably and value their souls cheaply."[8]

In another portion of the text, students learn that martyrdom does not entail death at all, but rather a transformation to a much improved form of eternal life. Here the textbooks engage in a complete reversal of the notions of life and death. Life is portrayed as a temporary and unhappy condition, inherently less blissful than the glorious eternal "life" awaiting the believer after death. Choosing martyrdom is not choosing a violent end to one's life; in fact, the whole notion of physical pain accompanying a violent martyrdom is ignored. Martyrdom is simply a choice to transform life into a different state, where the believer joins his fellow martyrs. As a ninth-grade Islamic education textbook explains:

> Martyrdom is, in fact, a transition to another life that is refined and pure from all worries and sorrows . . . . The martyrs, through their overwhelming joy in the Hereafter, wish that their brothers in [this] world would wage *Jihad*, become martyrs themselves, and win *Allah*'s good will."[9]

However, although martyrdom is supposed to be a voluntary act, in the fifth grade the students learn that the profitable deal is not exactly a matter of free choice. Indeed, children discover that *Allah* severely punishes those who refuse to accept the deal. Together with persuading children to recognize the profitability of the deal, Syrian textbooks take no chances, threatening and scaring them into developing a willingness to die. In the fifth grade the students learn that "fleeing from the battle is a grave crime that entails heavy punishment in this world as well as in the Hereafter."[10] That threat is repeated in the ninth grade, when students are told that "evasion of

Jihad and disrespect of the liberation of the homeland are high treason which will be costly in this world and in the Hereafter."[11]

Material Rewards

To mobilize its students to wage *Jihad* against the enemy, the Syrian education system does more than just offer divinely ordained rewards. It also promises benefits in this world, to be delivered by the Syrian state. The textbooks teach the children that Syrian president Hafez Al-Assad "believes in the [elevated] status of the martyrs . . . and provides them and their families with much attention."[12] A ninth-grade textbook explains that this presidential care is expressed, for example, in the establishment of a special Syrian city by Hafez Al-Assad called "The City of the Martyrs' Children." In that city, the children of the martyrs "acquire knowledge and . . . receive compensation for the motherly and fatherly love they have lost."[13]

With the rewards they receive from the state, the family members of a martyr enjoy an enviable status in Syrian society. The comforting knowledge that the state will care for the families they leave behind further promotes the notion that martyrdom is a beneficial deal. A martyr's death bestows on his family not only material benefits but also great honor. A story presented in a textbook for the fifth grade illustrates that point. It tells the tale of an orphaned girl whose father was killed in the war and who became a pupil at the "Martyrs' Children School" established by the Syrian president. The girl explains her privileged status to a visiting cousin:

> It is true that I lost my father, but I found in our President Hafez Al-Assad the father that embraces us all with his noble heart. The revolution provided all of us with the feeling of a happy family and enabled us to be educated properly. It put us on the road to a glorious future . . .
>
> The orphaned girl's visiting cousin responded: "your life is so beautiful."[14]

Society as a whole, tenth-grade Syrian children learn, must participate in bestowing respect and privileges on the families of martyrs. Such participation is central as an expression of "how much we love martyrdom."[15] Syrian society is thus conditioned to adopt the values of *Jihad* and martyrdom and to participate in turning those values into the cornerstones of its culture.

Martyrdom and the Arab-Israeli Conflict

After acquiring the theoretical principles of *Jihad* and martyrdom, the students begin the phase of their education that concerns practical implementation. Theory turns into reality when the children learn that their martyrdom must be carried out in the theater of the Arab-Israeli conflict. *Jihad,* teaches a fifth-grade textbook, must be waged against Israel, to liberate the Muslim land from blasphemous oppression. The book explains:

> [*Allah*'s reward for Martyrdom] recently prompted many youngsters to strive for death, in order to secure life to their nation. You can see them rush toward death, competing for it, in order to liberate their homes and homeland occupied by the Zionists and defiled by cruel imperialists . . . guarding the Muslims' land and liberating it from the profaned imperialists is the duty of all Muslims.[16]

A year later, in the sixth grade, children learn again that *Jihad* must be waged against Israel. Here, the text speaks in pan-Islamic (rather than pan-Arab) terms about the struggle that all Muslims must carry out against Israel to liberate the holy places of Islam from any Jewish presence. The text describes *Jihad* against Israel as a religious duty and warns the children that *Allah* will not forgive those who evade it. It also speaks of purifying Palestine of Jews:

> Muslims throughout the world struggle to expel the Jews from Palestine and to protect the Al-Aqsa Mosque. There is no forgiveness for whoever avoids *Jihad* in the cause of *Allah* for the purification of Palestine from the Jews. The purification of Palestine from the Jews in order to protect the Al-Aqsa Mosque is a *Jihad* for *Allah*.[17]

To emphasize the message, the same book instructs students to recite the following lines, wherein they are reminded of their duty as Muslims to wage *Jihad* against Israel, of the blessedness of dying for *Allah*, and of the benefits awaiting them after such a death:

Muslims throughout the world are preparing for *Jihad* against the Jews
and for their expulsion from Palestine . . . .
It is so wonderful to die for *Allah.*
Those who die for the cause of *Allah,* live with their God in Paradise.[18]

Tales of Martyrdom and Heroism

Attempting to deepen children's commitment to wage *Jihad* against
the Jews, the Syrian curriculum presents many stories about Syrians,
Lebanese, and Palestinians who were killed while carrying out attacks
on Israel. That the stories include tales of Lebanese and Palestinian
martyrs—not just Syrian ones—emphasizes the pan-Arab, Ba'athist
ideology and the pan-Arab nature of the war against Israel. One example is that of Nazih Qubrusli, a young Lebanese who died in the
process of waging *Jihad* against Israeli soldiers in Lebanon:

[Nazih Qubrusli] . . . refused to let the Zionists pollute his Lebanese
homeland. One morning . . . he waited for an Israeli patrol with the
intent of throwing grenades at it and causing disaster to the soldiers of
the cruel enemy. When an Israeli patrol passed by, he started killing the
enemy soldiers one after the other. . . . But . . . he died as a martyr, loyal
to his homeland, his country, and his Arab nation. His story has become a tremendous example of heroism and self-sacrifice. . . . So, we
can see that martyrdom is the way to break the aggression and the
occupiers.[19]

The Syrian curriculum presents Nazih Qubrusli's suicide attack on
Israeli soldiers in Lebanon as a story of ideal patriotism, heroism,
and self-sacrifice. The extent of one's love of country, Syrian children
learn, is expressed directly by one's hatred of his enemy and one's
willingness to kill its people—even at the price of one's own life. Martyrdom is not only a personal act of sacrifice; it also has national political importance. According to the Syrian education system, it is the
most effective tool of warfare and the best way to break the enemy's
confidence and spirit. As a heroic act of selflessness, martyrdom becomes a matter of both individual honor and happiness. That is dem-
onstrated in a speech by President Assad, quoted by a sixth-grade
textbook: "We will feel honorable and happy only to the extent to

which martyrdom becomes an inseparable part of our mental and physical existence."[20]

The story of Sana Muheidaly offers another example of the Syrian educational system's use of the martyrs to teach children to aspire for *Jihad*. It is recounted in *Social Education for the Sixth Grade*. Muheidaly, a seventeen-year-old girl, drove a truck full of explosives into a convoy of Israeli military trucks, tanks, armored vehicles, and soldiers, blowing up the truck and herself, and causing many Israeli deaths. The book quotes President Assad saying of Muheidaly, who died a few days before her wedding, "She married martyrdom."[21] The book also reports that President Assad "named a school in Damascus after Muheidaly." That, the text makes clear, is the usual way the Syrian state honors the memory of its martyrs.[22] The Syrian curriculum also endorses the memory of Dalal Al-Maghribi, a twenty-year-old woman who died during a 1978 attack on an Israeli civilian bus.[23]

Syrian children learn about the importance of self-sacrifice and martyrdom through the description of the Deir Yassin massacre in 1948. That massacre, in which an armed Jewish unit attacked the Palestinian village of Deir Yassin and killed many of its citizens, is traditionally invoked as part of the Arab version of the "1948 disaster," and in the context of exposing the Israeli attempt to expel the Arab population from Palestine. In the Syrian textbooks, however, the Deir Yassin massacre becomes a heroic battle, during which there were many examples of martyrdom.

One such example, appearing in a tenth-grade textbook, describes the bravery of the women who participated in the battle alongside the men. Among them was Hulwa Zaydan, who "pushed her husband and son to the battlefield and when they became martyrs, screamed with joy and hurried to join the battle and fight the aggressors."[24] Zaydan, continues the book, kept fighting until she was killed, "and watered her country's soil with her blood."[25] Similarly, a young villager, Abd Al-Hamid, "penetrated the enemy's lines, threw bombs at them, and fought them with cold weapons until he died and became a martyr [fulfilling] his duty."[26] These and similar casualties at Deir Yassin are described by the book as "casualties of honor [which] mark the heroism of the Arab and his steadfastness against . . . the plunderers who want to occupy his land."[27] The authors of this textbook add the expected conclusion: "And so you can see that martyrdom is deeply rooted in the Arab soul and they fulfill it with force and determination."[28]

Child-Warriors

Martyrdom is not something that the Syrian education system believes should be limited to adults. Children must not only be educated in, but must themselves directly participate in and carry out *Jihad*. For that reason, the textbooks devote much attention to creating a myth of child-warriors. According to the books, these are Arab children of supreme qualities and bravery, who chose to participate in the battle against the Israeli enemy and risk or sacrifice their lives in the process. Their actions are to be studied and emulated as great acts of patriotism and martyrdom.

The myth of the child-warrior is embraced by the Syrian curriculum at a very early level. A fifth-grade reader, for example, devotes a whole chapter to "The Little *Fedai* [one who sacrifices himself]." The chapter describes Palestinian camps in which young children are given military training and learn to become young warriors. It claims that such training turns Palestinian children into effective fighters, ready to defeat the Zionist enemy:

> In one of the camps of the young Sons of Palestine, Ayham is training in carrying weapons and he and his little friends are preparing to participate in the liberation of their country. . . .
>
> The children in the camps learn to use light weapons and fight with cold weapons. Their instructor is pleased to see that they learn the martial arts just as they learn their [regular] lessons. . . . Each year, regiments of youth come out from the camps of the Palestinian revolution. Time passes and they grow up and lead courageous *Fedai* operations, defeat the enemy, set fire to his tanks and armored cars, and terrorize the enemy soldiers' hearts, until the enemy ultimately realizes that the plunderer will not survive and the land belongs to its owner.[29]

Syrian students also learn about Arab children's role in the fight against Israel from their *Reader for the Sixth Grade*. In "The Three Heroes," this textbook relates the story of three Palestinian children who initiated an operation against Israeli forces. One child spilled oil on the road where "the enemy's trucks" were passing, another poured sugar in the gas tanks of "the enemy's cars," and a third changed the sign-posts on the road.[30] The book explains that later, the Voice of Palestine Radio announced that "the *Fedais* have managed to blow up an enemy weapons factory."[31] The credit for the successful operation was given to the children whose deeds prevented the enemy's forces from reaching the site. The reader then asks Syrian children to draw direct personal lessons from this story. Two of the questions posed in the assignment following the tale of the three heroes are, "Do you think that defending the homeland is relevant only to adults?" and "What is your part in defending your homeland?"[32]

The idea that children must directly and personally commit *Jihad* is repeated in a sixth- grade social education textbook. The book glorifies "the path of *Shahadah*" [martyrdom][33] as the path of truth, justice, and glory.[34] It claims that it cannot count all the names of the young boys and girls who died as martyrs, there are so many of them.[35] It teaches the students to admire the child-warriors who gave their lives to the Arab cause:

> [We] admire and respect the young male and female martyrs, [we give] absolute love [to them]. . . . [We pledge] full commitment to the young male and female martyrs to follow their path. The *Shahadah* is the supreme value. [36]

After reading about these young martyrs, the children again review the principles and ideas of the *Shahadah*. They are reminded of their personal obligation to become martyrs and are told, again, that death by martyrdom is only a transformation into a better, more noble, and eternal life. They also learn that *Shahadah*—martyrdom—must be an inseparable part of their physical existence:

> You are at the forefront of those who must sanctify the *Shahadah* and carry its flag. . . . The *Shahadah* is an inseparable part of our physical and mental entity and it can lead it altogether. . . . The *Shahadah* is the continuation of life and life's most noble and pure form. The *Shahadah* is merely a qualitative transformation from one chapter of narrow life to a much broader unlimited life. The *Shahadah* is eternity and the martyr is eternal and alive forever and ever.[37]

At the end of that review, the book exhorts the children to desire martyrdom at an early age and to prefer it to life: "Let us desire martyrdom, for it is eternity, let us bless the martyrs, let us aspire for their path always."[38]

The attention devoted by Syrian textbooks to the idea that even children must wage *Jihad* reflects the regime's aspiration for a totally mobilized society. The struggle against Israel is seen as so great that it demands participation from all sectors of Arab society: men, women, and children. Children are most directly exposed to the regime's expectations. The message, presented in various ways, is always the same: martyrdom is the personal and immediate duty of every child. Any member of society, of any age, is a soldier whose very life is secondary to achieving the goals of the regime.

In educating children to strive for martyrdom, the Syrian education system teaches them to cherish death, rather than life. It is the ultimate subjugation of children's spirits. While very young, they discover that their society values them more as martyrs than as living children. They are lured to martyrdom with promises of divine and earthly rewards; they are threatened with punishment if they shirk this duty; and they are indoctrinated with myths of adults and children waging *Jihad* in the recent past. In this education, the Syrian state acts as the enemy of its own youth, exhorting them to die at the altar of their pan-Arab nationalist state.

Notes

1. *Islamic Education for the Fourth Grade, 1998–1999,* for example, states on page 44: "*Jihad* is a religious duty for all Muslims, even if the number of their enemies is double [their own]."

2. *Islamic Education for the Fifth Grade, 1998–1999,* p. 59.

3. *Islamic Education for the Fourth Grade, 1998–1999,* p. 45.

4. *The Koran,* Surat Al-Tauba, verse 111.

5. *Islamic Education for the Fourth Grade, 1998–1999,* p. 46.

6. Ibid., p. 56.

7. Ibid.

8. *Islamic Education for the Fifth Grade, 1998–1999,* p. 108.

9. *Islamic Education for the Ninth Grade, 1999–2000,* p. 41.

10. *Islamic Education for the Fifth Grade, 1998–1999,* p. 59.

11. Ibid., p. 108.

12. *Islamic Education for the Ninth Grade, 1999–2000,* p. 41.

13. Ibid.

14. *Reader for the Fifth Grade, Part I, 1998–1999,* p. 42.

15. *National [Pan-Arab] Socialist Education for the Tenth Grade, 1998–1999,* p. 152.

16. *Islamic Education for the Fifth Grade, 1998–1999,* p. 108.

17. *Islamic Education for the Sixth Grade, 1998–1999*, p. 57
18. Ibid., p. 58
19. *Social Education for the Sixth Grade, 1998–1999*, p. 115.
20. Ibid.
21. Ibid., p. 116.
22. Ibid., p. 117.
23. *Reader for the Sixth Grade, Part II, 1999–2000*, p. 97.
24. *Social Education for the Fifth Grade, 1998–1999*, p. 110.
25. Ibid.
26. Ibid.
27. Ibid., p. 111.
28. Ibid.
29. *Reader for the Fifth Grade, Part I, 1998–1999*, p. 109.
30. *Reader for the Sixth Grade, Part I, 1999–2000*, p. 149.
31. Ibid., p. 151.
32. Ibid., p. 152.
33. The *Shahadah* has two, interrelated meanings in Islam. The word *Shahadah* refers to the uttering of the "testimony" that turns a man into a Muslim: "There is no God but *Allah* and Muhammad is his Messenger." The second meaning of *Shahadah* is "martyrdom."
34. *Social Education for the Sixth Grade, 1998–1999*, p. 118.
35. Ibid.
36. Ibid., p. 119.
37. Ibid., pp. 119–20.
38. Ibid., p. 120.

7

Anti-Semitism
in the Syrian Curriculum

Syrian textbooks, especially in the fields of history and Islamic education, employ anti-Semitic imagery to describe the character and behavior of Jews. Here, the books go beyond the political struggle with Israel and Zionism to evoke European and other traditional anti-Semitic motifs, including those of Islamic theological origins.[1] Islamic education textbooks, whose focal point is the affirmation of Ba'athist ideas (including the struggle against Israel), deal with much more than the Islamic past. As with the teaching of *Jihad,* where the secular Syrian state utilizes Islamic principles to serve its present-day political goal of fighting Israel, religious Islamic anti-Semitism is used to instill in students a unifying religious hatred toward a national enemy. In most cases, students are asked to project the "Jewish behavior" portrayed in a theological context onto contemporary "Zionist Jews" and their conduct in the Arab-Israeli conflict.[2]

Syrian students are introduced to Islamic anti-Semitism by the sixth grade. *Islamic Education for the Sixth Grade* tells, under the heading "The Treachery of the Jews," the stories of the dispute between the Prophet Muhammad and the three Jewish tribes of the city of Al-Madinah: Banu Nadhir, Banu Quraydha, and Banu Qaynuqa'.[3]

The stories describe the Jews of Al-Madinah as the enemies of Islam and Muslims. They claim that the Jews tried regularly to attack

Muslims and to instigate rifts among them, concocting lies to sway them from Islam. They betrayed the Muslims, and even tried to assassinate the Prophet Muhammad. As an example of such Jewish behavior, this sixth-grade text tells the story of a Muslim woman who went to a Jewish goldsmith to sell him some gold jewelry. Along the way some Jews gathered around her, and abused her. The Jews, portrayed here as haters of Muslims, aggressive, and cruel, were punished for their actions by the Prophet Muhammad. In retaliation, he besieged the Jewish tribe of Banu Qaynuqa', to which the attackers belonged, until they surrendered. Later, the book reports, he banished them from the city.[4]

Further demonstrating the contemptible nature of Jews, the book tells a story of the banishment of yet another Jewish tribe, dating from early Islamic history. It describes a meeting between the Prophet Muhammad and the leaders of the Jewish Banu Nadhir tribe. The Prophet became suspicious of his Jewish hosts because he "sensed the spark of treachery in some of their eyes."[5] His intuition was correct; some of the Jews had entered a neighboring house, intending to throw a rock and kill him. After leaving the place, the Prophet expelled the Banu Nadhir tribe from Al-Madinah as punishment for their betrayal. He gave them ten days forewarning, after which those who stayed would be executed.[6]

Following that expulsion, the only Jews left in the city of Al-Madinah were the Banu Quraydha. They, too, were banished from the Arab Peninsula after having committed an act of treason during the Battle of the Ditch. After that, the region was cleared of Jews.[7]

The story of the banishment of the Jewish tribes forms an integral part of Islamic tradition, and parts of it are retold in this book and in many others. In all of them the Jews are described as a homogeneous group typically prone to betrayal and treachery. This element of Islamic tradition appears in another sixth-grade history textbook about the era of the Prophets and the righteous Caliphs.[8] It tells the story of the treachery and subsequent banishment of the Khaybar Jews, along with similar stories about the Jews of Al-Madinah. The Khaybar Jews were expelled by the Prophet Muhammad, "who felt it was high time to punish the Jews for their deception and treachery."[9] Here, the equation between the corrupt qualities of Jews in Islamic tradition and in present-day Arab-Israeli politics is spelled out directly. After being exposed to "the Jews' treachery to the Prophet Muhammad," the students are asked "to compare the Jews' position toward the Prophet at that time with the Zionists' position toward the Arab nation today."[10]

Endorsing a similar view, *Islamic Education for the Eleventh Grade* makes general statements about the Jewish character and conduct. The book claims that Jews hated Muslims and incited hostility against them because of religious envy—because Muhammad proved that prophecy was not a purely Jewish domain:

> The Jews spare no effort to deceive us, hate us, deny our Prophet, incite against us, and distort the holy scriptures.
>
> The Jews cooperate with the Polytheist and the infidels against the Muslims because they know Islam reveals their crafty ways and abject characteristics.
>
> One of the reasons for the Jews' hostility to the Arabs is that *Allah* sent Muhammad, the last of the prophets, from amongst the Arabs, while they thought prophecy was solely their domain.[11]

After reading that text, students are instructed to list the adjectives used by *The Koran* to describe the Jews, and to clarify the reasons for the Jews' hostility toward the Arabs.[12]

By tying ancient Islamic tradition to the present time, Syrian textbooks teach that there is a unique and homogenous Jewish character that has remained unchanged throughout the ages. How, then, could there be any hope for Jewish-Muslim or Jewish-Arab reconciliation? The only method these textbooks suggest for dealing with the Jews is the one employed by Muhammad—to extirpate the evil and treachery by expelling or killing the Jews. This form of anti-Semitism covers the broadly negative qualities of every member of the Jewish religion. As a text for the tenth grade explains, the Jews who double-crossed the Prophet and the Muslims are "traitors in all times and places. . . . [This character is] rooted in the Jewish personality."[13] For that reason, coexistence with Jews is "dangerous and threatens the Arab and Islamic existence."[14]

"The logic of justice," concludes the book, "obligates the application of the single verdict [on the Jews] from which there is no escape; namely, that their criminal intentions be turned against them and that they be exterminated. The duty of Muslims of our time is to pull themselves together, unite their ranks, and wage war on their enemy until *Allah* hands down his judgement on them and us."[15]

Syrian textbooks employ anti-Semitic historical and theological motifs not only for the sake of nurturing hatred toward the Jews but also to lead students to the inevitable and practical conclusion: the Jews, "the enemies of *Allah*," are of an unchangeable and historically dangerous nature that defies peaceful coexistence. They must be exterminated, and the Muslims and Arabs of today must wage war to fulfill this mission.

Notes

1. For example, the "arrogant, greedy, and disloyal" character attributed by the Syrian textbooks to the Jews is used to justify the Holocaust as something the Jews brought upon themselves, "because of their inability to assimilate in the societies in which they lived, their control and monopoly of money exchanges, banking, and finance, and because of their betrayal of their homeland Germany, when they leagued themselves with the Allies in WWII." *National [Pan-Arab] Socialist Education for the Tenth Grade, 1998–1999*, p. 104.

2. Syrian textbooks also draw upon non-Islamic Anti-Semitic motifs, such as blaming the Jews for the crucifixion of Jesus. *Islamic Education for the Sixth Grade* tells the story as it is told by Muslim tradition. According to this version, the Jews tried to crucify Jesus, but *Allah* saved him from the traps they had set for him. 1998–1999, p. 56.

3. *Islamic Education for the Sixth Grade, 1998–1999*, p. 93.

4. Ibid.

5. Ibid., p. 195.

6. Ibid.

7. Ibid.

8. *History—The Era of the Prophets and the Righteous Caliphs for the Sixth Grade, 1999–2000*. The "righteous Caliphs" were the first four Caliphs who led Islam after the death of Muhammad: Abu Bakr, 'Umar, 'Uthman, and 'Ali.

9. Ibid., p. 55.

10. Ibid., p. 51.

11. *Islamic Education for the Eleventh Grade, 1999–2000*, p. 33.

12. Ibid., p. 34.

13. *Islamic Education for the Tenth Grade, 1999-2000*, p. 115.

14. Ibid.

15. Ibid.

8

Conclusions

This survey of Syrian textbooks, which covers the fourth through eleventh grades, offers us a glimpse into how difficult it will be for the Ba'athist regime to come to terms and a reconciliation with Israel and the Jewish people. It is a difficulty of its own making. The Ba'athist classroom is the organ through which Syrian children are shaped into young warriors and useful members of society. There they are taught the proper way in which to understand such varying subjects as the inimical and treacherous ways of Israel and the West, the wonders of revolution, steadfastness in war, and the beauty of death through martyrdom.

To exorcize a single idea from within an incoherent, and therefore, unrelated and unintegrated mass of ideas can be easily accomplished after a peace treaty. Unfortunately, the ideas which are inculcated into Syrian children are not such an incoherent mass of reflections on Israel and the "colonialist" West. They reflect an integrated totalitarian ideology that is anchored, ultimately, to relentless conflict with Israel and the West. For Syria cannot exorcize its hostile treatment of Israel from its school curriculum in isolation from an overall transformation of the ideology that informs Syria's Ba'athist regime, society, and culture.

To accept a new, pluralistic basis to regional politics would ultimately force the regime to abandon its dream of pan-Arab unity from the Atlantic to the Indian Ocean—a dream which cannot accept Israel's existence. To jettison its ferocious enmity toward Israel and the West would force the Syrian regime to abandon its focus on the danger of a relentless, cunning, and subversive enemy. To relinquish its focus on the omnipresent, lurking dangers of such an enemy, would strip the Syrian regime of the cause for the perpetual state of conflict and *Jihad*. To abandon the perpetual state of conflict and *Jihad* would deny the regime its demand for sacrifice of society. It would deny the regime its excuse for Syria's economic hardships. It would deny the regime the foundations of martial law and state of emergency. And it would deny the regime the justification for the absolute control the Syrian state has over the private lives of even its children. Without that control and that state of emergency, the regime would lose the means to sustain a state of perpetual revolution in Syrian society. In short, a real peace with Israel would demand a profound transformation of the very ideology and structure of the Ba'athist regime. Removing any element of this complex chain of interrelated ideas will shake the foundations of Syria's Ba'athist regime.

Syria's educational system performs the state's initial engagement and indoctrination of youth into Ba'athist ideology. From this ideology emerges the intensity of the hatred of Israel, the West, and the Jews. At the same time, it exposes the fragility of the Ba'athist system because its ideology has trapped Syria into a war it cannot afford and a peace its regime cannot survive.

Appendix

Attached are selections from the original Arabic texts, along with their translations as quoted in the study.

الجمهورية العربية السورية

وزارة التربية

التربية القومية الاشتراكية

الأول الثانوي

١٤١٩ هـ ـ ١٩٩٨ ـ ١٩٩٩م

المؤسسة العامة للمطبوعات والكتب المدرسية

الدرس الرابع عشر:

الحركة الصهيونية

أولاً ـ ظهور الحركة الصهيونية:

بعد ظهور الاستعمار، وسيطرة الـدول الأوربيـة علـى كثير مـن أراضي البلـدان المتخلفة، سعى بعض المفكرين من أغنياء اليهود مع الدول الاستعمارية إلى إيجـاد كيـان يجمع يهود العالم، وتكوين مستعمرات خاصة بهم، فاستقر رأيهـم علـى استعمار أرض فلسطين لتكون منطلقاً لهم من أجل السيطرة على الوطن العربي، ونهب ثرواته، وجعلـه مجالاً لاستثمار أموالهم، ولتحقيـق ذلـك تم تشكيل حركـة سميّت بالحركـة الصهيونيـة، وحددت هدفها في إنشاء وطن قومي لليهود في فلسطين العربية.

تعريف الصهيونية:

الصهيونية حركة سياسية عنصرية استعمارية استيطانية عدوانية توسعية ٠٠ ٠ ملة بالاستعمار. تسخّر الدين اليهودي لتحقيق أهدافها في إقامـة وطن قومـي لليهـود في فلسطين والأراضي المجاورة لها.

ثانياً ـ عوامل ظهور الحركة الصهيونية:

لقد ظهرت الحركة الصهيونية نتيجة عوامل متعددة منها:

١ ـ الدعم الاستعماري:

نشأت الحركة الصهيونية في القرن /١٩/ في أوربـا، وأصبحـت حليفـ الاستعمار الأوربي الذي حاول استكمال السيطرة على العالم أجمع.

٢ ـ استغلال الشعور اليهودي بالاضطهاد:

عملت الحركة الصهيونية على استخدام الدين اليهودي كعامل لجمع شتات اليهود في العالم، الذين ينتمون إلى قوميات مختلفة وشعوب متعددة للتخلص من حـ عزـ ي

After the rise of colonialism and the European states' takeover of many of the lands in underdeveloped countries, some thinkers among the rich Jews, together with the colonialist states, wanted to create an entity in which they could gather all the Jews of the world and establish settlements for them. They had their mind set on settling in the land of Palestine, which will be a starting point for them in order to take over [the entirety of] the Arab homeland, to rob its treasures and to convert it into a site in which their money could be invested. In order to accomplish this, a movement called "the Zionist movement" was established. . . .

Source: *National (Pan-Arab) Socialist Education for the Tenth Grade,* 1998–1999, p. 89.

... «خطر الحركة الصهيونية» ...

إن اليهود الصهاينة لا يكفون عن مهاجمة النازية واستغلال أعمالها لتبرير أعمالها. لكن أين هو الفارق بين جوهر النازية وجوهر الصهيونية، إن النازيين كانوا يدّعون التفوق العنصري والصهاينة يدّعون أنهم شعب ا لله المختار، يجب أن يخضع له جميع شعوب العالم... النازيون برروا احتلال أراضي الغير واستعبادهم لحاجتهم إلى المجال الحيوي: والصهاينة يحتلون أراضي الغير تحت ستار ضمان المجال الأمني للدولة التي أقاموها ظلماً وعدواناً على أراضي الغير، النازيون اضطهدوا وشردوا الشعوب الأخرى والصهاينة يفعلون الشيء نفسه اليوم مع العرب، وغداً مع الشعوب الإسلامية الأخرى وغيرها، إذا لم يتم وضع حد نهائي لإجرامهم وخرقهم المواثيق والأعراف والقوانين الدولية...

... من كلمة الرفيق الأمين العام حافظ الأسد
في مؤتمر القمة الإسلامي الخامس المنعقد في الكويت
... ١٩٨١/١/٢٧ م ...

The Zionist Jews do not cease to attack Nazism and exploit its actions in order to justify their own. But what is the difference between the essence of Nazism and Zionism? The Nazis claimed racial superiority and the Zionists claim they are *Allah*'s chosen people, who all other nations must be subjugated to. The Nazis justified their occupation of other's lands and their enslavement by claiming that they needed *lebensraum.* The Zionists occupy other people's lands under the guise of guaranteeing the security borders of the state which they established out of wrongdoing and through aggression against other [people's] lands. The Nazis persecuted and exiled other nations and the Zionists are doing the same today to the Arabs, and will tomorrow do it to the Islamic nations, and the rest of the nations, if an end will not be put to their crimes and to their violations of agreements, norms, and international laws.

Source: *National (Pan-Arab) Socialist Education for the Tenth Grade,* 1998–1999, p. 93.

٦ ـ تغاضت الحكومة البريطانية عـن نشـاط المنظمات الإرهابية الصهيونية مثـل "إرغون، وشتيرن" التي ارتكبت الفظائع ضد السكان العرب الآمنين عام ١٩٤٨ م.

ثالثاً ـ مرحلة الحرب العالمية الثانية:

استطاعت الصهيونية أن تسخر ظروف الحرب العالمية الثانية لصالحها من خلال:

١ ـ تشكيلها للفيلق العسكري، الذي حارب إلى جانب الحلفاء وأصبح فيمـا بعد نواة للجيش الإسرائيلي.

٢ ـ استغلال الاضطهاد النازي: لقد اضطهدت النازية خلال الحرب العالمية الثانيـة ملايين البشر في أوربا وغيرها، وقد أصاب جزء من هـذا الاضطهـاد اليهـود وللأسبـاب التالية:

آ ـ بحكم عدم اندماجهم بالشعوب والمجتمعات التي يعيشون بينها.

ب ـ لتسلطهم واحتكارهم المبادلات النقدية والمصارف والتمويل التجاري.

جـ ـ خيانتهم لوطنهم ألمانيا حيث وضعوا أنفسهم في خدمة الحلفاء.

واستطاعت الحركة الصهيونية توظيف هـذه العوامـل في السـاحة الأوربيـة كسبـاً للعطف عليهم.

٣ ـ نقل مركز النشاط الصهيوني مـن بريطانيـا إلى الولايـات المتحـدة الأمريكيـة: نتيجة لخروج بريطانيا من الحرب العالمية الثانية منهكة القوى. توجـه زعمـاء الصهيونيـة إلى الولايات المتحدة الأمريكية التي بدت قـوة كبرى بعد الحرب العالمية الثانية، ولها مصالحها الحيوية في الوطن العربي، لذلك بدأت حلقـات التلاحـم الأمريكـي الصهيونـي تتكامل منذ ذلك الحين ممثلة بـ: ـ المجلس الأمريكي الصهيوني عـام ١٩٤١ م الـذي هدف إلى تدعيم العلاقات الأمريكيـة الصهيونيـة. ـ عقـد مؤتمر صهيونـي في نيويورك (بلتيمور) عام ١٩٤٢ م الذي صدر عنـه وثيقة تضمنت استمرازية الهجرة اليهودية،

For example, the "arrogant, greedy and disloyal" character attributed by the Syrian textbooks to the Jews is used to justify the Holocaust as something the Jews brought upon themselves, "because of their inability to assimilate in the societies in which they lived, their control and monopoly of money exchanges, banking, and finance and because of their betrayal of their homeland Germany, when they leagued themselves with the Allies in WWII."

Source: *National (Pan-Arab) Socialist Education for the Tenth Grade,* 1998–1999, p. 104.

الجمهورية العربية السورية
وزارة التربية

التربية القومية الاشتراكية

الثاني الإعدادي

١٤٢٠هـ
١٩٩٩ـ٢٠٠٠م

المؤسسة العامة للمطبوعات والكتب المدرسية

للمطالعـــة:

الحركـــــة الصهيونية

إن الصراع بين الأمة العربية والحركة الصهيونية صراع قاسٍ ومريـــر ومديـــد، وماذلك إلا لأن هذه الحركة العنصرية النازية ترمي إلى استعمار رقعة مـــن الوطـــن العربي تمتد من الفرات إلى النيل، استعماراً استيطانياً بربرياً على حساب الأمة العربيـــة، ووجودها القومي في أرضها ووطنها، وهذا الاستعمار الصهيوني المدعوم مـــن قبـــل الأمبريالية العالمية وعلى رأسها الولايات المتحدة الأمريكية أشبه شيء بسرطان خبيـــث فتّاك، نشب في جزء من قلب الوطن العربي- فلسطين المحتلة- ويحاول أن يمتد ويترعرع على حساب الأجزاء الأخرى من الوطن العربي وعلى حساب الأمة العربية ككل.

وبذلك يصبح الوجود الاستعماري الاستيطاني الصهيوني في الجزء المحتـــل مـــن فلسطين على طرفي نقيض مع وجود الأمة العربية في أرضها ووطنها، ويشكل عقبـــة في طريق نزوع الأمة العربية إلى تحقيق وحدتها وتطوير إمكاناتها، وبلوغ ماتصبو إليه مـــن تقدم ورقي لتحتل المكانة اللائقة بما بين أمم الأرض في عالمنا المعاصر.

وإذا كان الصراع بين الأمة العربية والصهيونية قد بدأ فعلاً منـــــذ أن بـــدأت شراذم شذاذ الآفاق تتوافد إلى ربوع فلسطين منذ أواخر القرن التاسع عشـــر وأوائـــل القرن العشرين، فإنه قد تبلور وتجسد في أربعة حروب خاضتها الأمة العربية ضد العـــدو

This Zionist imperialism . . . is similar to a malignant and lethal cancer which broke out in part of the heart of the Arab homeland—occupied Palestine—and is trying to spread into other parts of the Arab homeland at the expense of the Arab nation as a whole. By so doing, the Zionist colonialist . . . existence in the occupied part of Palestine totally negates the existence of the Arab nation on its land, becoming a stumbling block before the Arab nation [preventing it from] fulfilling its unity and developing its resources. . . .

Source: *National (Pan-Arab) Socialist Education for the Eighth Grade,* 1999–2000, p. 96.

٥- الإبقاء على التخلف والتوتر:

إن وجود إسرائيل في قلب الوطن العربي جعل المنطقة في حالة توتر دائم، ودفـــع العرب إلى تخصيص جزء كبير من ثرواتهم للمجهود الحربي، مما يبطئ القيـــام بأعمـــال التنمية والتصنيع وتوفير الخدمات الصحية والاقتصادية والتعليمية للمواطنين، ويؤدي هذا الوضع إلى التخلف مما يسهل على الاستعمار الإبقاء على سيطرته واستغلاله. غـــير أن العرب الذين أخذوا بأسباب العلم والعمل مستعدون أيضاً لإنفـــاق جمـــيع ثروالهـــم للتخلص من الخطر الذي يهدد وجودهم.

ولهذا تعمل سورية في ظل ثورة حزب البعث العربي الاشتراكي وبقيادة الرفيـــق المناضل حافظ الأسد على حشد الطاقات العربيـــة لتصفيـــة الوجـــود الاستعماري الاستيطاني الصهيوني في الأرض العربية وتحرير كامل التراب العربي المحتل. وقـــد عبّر الرفيق المناضل حافظ الأسد عن ذلك بقوله:

"إننا نواجه في الصراع العربي الإسرائيلي الحركة الصهيونية العالمية، هذه الحركـــة العنصرية التوسعية العدوانية التي أنتجت غزواً استعمارياً، نفذته إسرائيل بدعـــم غـــير محدود من قوى.....الاستعمار".

. . . Syria operates in keeping with the revolution of the Arab Socialist Ba'ath party, and under the leadership of the comrade, the man of struggle, Hafez Al-Assad, to mass Arab resources in order to annihilate the Zionist colonialist existence in the Arab land and to liberate all the occupied Arab land. The comrade, the man of struggle, Hafez Al-Assad, expressed this by saying: "In the Arab-Israeli conflict we are struggling against the world Zionist movement. This is the racist, expansionist, and aggressive movement that gave birth to a colonialist invasion carried out by Israel with unlimited support by the colonialist forces."

The existence of Israel at the heart of the Arab homeland created a condition of permanent tension in the region and pushed the Arabs to allocate much of their resources to the war effort. This slows down the development and industrialization works . . . and leads to a backwardness which makes it easier for colonialism to maintain its control and exploitation. But the Arabs . . . are willing to use all their resources in order to rid themselves of the danger that threatens their existence.

Source: *National (Pan-Arab) Socialist Education for the Eighth Grade,* 1999–2000, p. 48.

الصهيوني العنصري عبر أعوام ١٩٤٨ - ١٩٥٦ - ١٩٦٧ - ١٩٧٣. وإن حرب تشرين التحريرية التي رفعت رأس العرب عالياً وأعادت الثقة إلى نفس المواطن العربي والجندي العربي، وأثبتت للعالم أجمع قدرة الأمة العربية على الصمود والمواجهة لتحرير أراضيها وطرد الغاصب المحتل، وكان لشعبنا العربي في هذا القطر بقيادة الرفيق المناضل حـــــافظ الأسد دور أساسي وفعال فيها، نقول إن هذه الحرب ليست خاتمة المطاف في الصـــراع العربي مع الصهيونية العنصرية،وإنما هي حلقة في سلسلة حروب تحريرية قد تكون مـــن نصيب أكثر من جيل من أجيال الأمة العربية حتى يتم تحرير كامل التراب المحتل،وحـــتى يصفى الوجود الاستعماري الاستيطاني الصهيوني في الأرض العربية.

من منهاج التثقيف الحزبي
الجزء الرابع "دراسات عامة"

٩٧

. . . This war is not the end of the Arab conflict with racist Zionism. It is but a chapter in a series of wars of liberation . . . until the occupied land is fully liberated and the Zionist colonialist settlement in the Arab land ends.

Source: *National (Pan-Arab) Socialist Education for the Eighth Grade,* 1999–2000, p. 97.

الجمهورية العربية السورية
وزارة التربية

القراءة

الجزء الثاني

الخامس الابتدائي

١٤١٩ هـ ـ ١٩٩٨ ـ ١٩٩٩ م
المؤسسة العامة للمطبوعات والكتب المدرسية

هَذِهِ أَرْضُنَا

١ ــ انتَهَتْ لَيْلَى مِنْ كِتَابَةِ وَظَائِفِها ، ثُمَّ نَهَضَتْ إلى أَبِيهَا وَأُمِّها وَقَالَتْ لَهُما :

ــ أَنَا ذَاهِبَةٌ إلى فِرَاشِي ، تُصْبِحانِ عَلَى خَيْرٍ .

لَمْ يَمْضِ عَلى نَوْمِها إلاَّ دَقَائِقُ حَتَّى سَمِعَتْ طَلَقَاتِ رَصَاصٍ كَثِيرَةً . نَهَضَتْ مِنْ فِرَاشِها مُضْطَرِبَةً ، حَاوَلَتْ إضَاءَةَ المِصْبَاحِ، لكنَّ التَّيَّارَ الكَهْرَبائيَّ كانَ مَقْطُوعاً . فَزَادَ قَلَقُها

ــ ٤٢ ــ

واضْطِرابُها ، وَسَمِعَتْ ضَجيجاً وأصْواتَ أُناسٍ يَدْخُلونَ
حَديقَةَ بَيْتِها ، فَتَحَتِ النَّافِذَةَ . فَرَأتْ في الظَّلامِ رجَالاً مُسَلَّحينَ
يَطْرُدُونَ أَباها وأُمها مِنَ البَيْتِ . قَالَتْ لَيْلى لِنَفْسِها : لاشَكَّ أنَّهُمْ
لُصُوصٌ ، وَمَا هِيَ إلاَّ لحَظَاتٌ، حَتَّى دَخَلُوا غُرْفَتَها ، وَقَالُوا
لَها بِلَهْجَةٍ جَافَّةٍ :

ـ هَيَّا ، اخْرُجِي أنْتِ أيْضاً مِنَ البَيْتِ ، قَالَتْ لَهُمْ :

ـ وَلَكِنَّ هَذا بَيْتُنا ، فَلِمَاذا تَطْرُدُونَنَا مِنْهُ ؟ قَالُوا :

ـ اُخْرُجِي ، وَلاَ تُنَاقِشِي . اُخْرُجِي بِسُرْعَةٍ وإلاَّ قَتَلْنَاكِ .

٢ ـ جَرُّوها مِنْ يَدِهَا بِقَسْوَةٍ ، وَكانَتْ مَعَهُمْ أسْلِحَةٌ كَثيرَةٌ ،
كَانَتْ وُجُوهُهُمْ عابِسَةً كَوُجُوهِ الشَّياطِينِ ، رَمَوْا لَيْلى في
الشَّارِعِ فَصَرَخَتْ :

ـ هَذا ظُلْمٌ ! هَذا احْتِلالٌ واغْتِصابٌ ، إنَّكُمْ تَطْرُدونَنَا مِنْ
بَيْتِنَا ، فَأيْنَ نَذْهَبُ لِنَعِيشَ ؟ ، قَالُوا لَها :

ـ اذْهَبُوا إلى الصَّحْراءِ ، وَعِيشُوا في خَيْمَةٍ ، اذْهَبُوا إلى الْجَحيمِ .
صَرَخَتْ لَيْلى غَاضِبَةٌ :

ـ لَنْ نَخَافَكُمْ ، سَنُدافِعُ عَنْ بَيْتِنا .

وَلَمْ تَشْعُرْ إلاَّ بِيَدِ أُمِّها تَهُزُّها وَتُوقِظُها مِنَ النَّوْمِ .

٣ ـ لَقَدْ كانَ حُلماً مُزْعِجاً ، وَقَصَّتْ عَلى والِدَيْها مارَأتْهُ في نَوْمِها .

ـ ٤٤ ـ

قَالَ الْوَالِدُ :

هٰذَا مَا حَدَثَ فِي فِلَسْطِينَ ، لَكِنَّهُ حَدَثَ فِي الْيَقَظَةِ لَا فِي النَّوْمِ يَا بُنَيَّتِي . لَقَدْ غَزَا أَرْضَنَا أُنَاسٌ غُرَبَاءُ ، جَاؤُوا مِنْ بِلَادٍ بَعِيدَةٍ وَمَعَهُمْ أَسْلِحَةٌ كَثِيرَةٌ ، فَطَرَدُوا أَهْلَهَا مِنْ بُيُوتِهِمْ ، وَقَعَدُوا فِيهَا مُحْتَلِّينَ غَاصِبِينَ .

قَالَتْ لَيْلَى :

وَلَكِنَّ هٰذَا ظُلْمٌ وَعُدْوَانٌ ! وَيَجِبُ أَلَّا نَسْكُتَ عَلَى الظُّلْمِ ، يَجِبُ أَنْ نُقَاتِلَ هٰؤُلَاءِ الْمُعْتَدِينَ حَتَّى نَسْتَرِدَّ وَطَنَنَا يَا أَبِي .

قَالَ الْأَبُ :

نَعَمْ يَا بُنَيَّتِي، نَحْنُ نُقَاتِلُ هٰؤُلَاءِ الصَّهَايِنَةَ الْمُعْتَدِينَ ، وَلَنْ نَسْكُتَ عَلَى الظُّلْمِ حَتَّى تَعُودَ فِلَسْطِينُ لِأَصْحَابِهَا ، وَيَعُودَ الْحَقُّ إِلَى أَهْلِهِ .

شَرْحُ الْمُفْرَدَاتِ

حَاقَةٌ: قَاسِيَةٌ، اِغْتِصَابٌ : أَخْذُ الشَّيْءِ قَسْرًا، نَسْتَرِدُّ : نَسْتَعِيدُ.

[In her dream Layla] heard voices of people entering the courtyard of her home . . . In the darkness she saw armed people expelling her father and mother from the house. Layla told herself: "these are surely thieves." Within several moments they entered her room and told her in a dry tone: "go ahead. Get out of the house."

She told them: "but this is our house. Why are you expelling us from it?"

They said: "get out without arguing. Get out quickly, otherwise we will kill you." They held her by the hand and dragged her violently. They had many weapons and their faces were angry like the face of Satan. They threw Layla in the street and she screamed: "this is an injustice, this is occupation, this is plundering. You are throwing us out of our home. Where will we live?"

They answered: "go to the desert and live there in a tent. Go to hell."

[Layla wakes up and discusses the dream with her father.]

Her father told her: "this is what actually took place in Palestine, but it happened, my daughter, in reality and not in a dream. Our land was invaded by foreigners who came from far away lands carrying many weapons. They expelled the people from their homes and settled in them as occupiers and robbers."

Layla said: "but this is an occupation and an aggression. We must not remain silent about this injustice. We must fight against these aggressors until we gain back our homeland, father."

Said the father: "Correct, my daughter. We fight against those Zionist aggressors and will not remain silent until we restore Palestine to its owners. . . ."

Source: *Reader for the Fifth Grade, Part II*, 1998–1999, pp. 43–45.

الجمهورية العربية السورية
وزارة التربية

القراءة

السادس الابتدائي

الجزء الثاني

١٤١٨هـ
١٩٩٧ - ١٩٩٨م

المؤسسة العامة للمطبوعات والكتب المدرسية

79

الشَّعْبِ الفِلَسْطِينِيِّ إلى وَطَنِهِ ، وَإعْطائِهِ حُقُوقَهُ ، وَلكِنَّ الدُّوَلَ الاسْتِعْمارِيَّةَ الَّتِي تُسانِدُ « إسْرائِيلَ » تَقِفُ حائِلاً دونَ تَحْقِيقِ هذا النِّداءِ .

إنَّ أَطْماعَ الْعَدُوِّ الصَّهْيُونِيِّ في فِلَسْطِين وَالأَرْضِ الْعَرَبِيَّةِ لَيْس لها نِهايَةٌ ، وَلا نَعْرِفُ أَيْنَ تَنْتَهِي هَذِهِ الأَطْماعُ . إنَّ الصَّهايِنَةَ لا يُفَكِّرُونَ في إعادَةِ الأَرْضِ الْمُغْتَصَبَةِ إلى أَهْلِها .

٣ – لَقَدْ ضَحَّى إخْوانُنا الفِلَسْطِينِيُّونَ بِدِمائِهِمْ حتَّى سَمِعَ العالَمُ كُلُّهُ صَوْتَهُمْ ، وَعَرَفَ قَضِيَّتَهُمْ ، وَمازالُوا يَمُوتُونَ في ساحَةِ الشَّرَفِ ، لكِنْ بَعْدَ أَنْ يُكَبِّدُوا الْعَدُوَّ خَسائِرَ جَسِيمَةً في أَرْواحِهِ وَمُمْتَلَكاتِهِ دِفاعاً عَنْ أَرْضِهِمْ .

وَيَجِبُ أَنْ نُضِيفَ إلى هذا الجِهادِ مُعاوَنَةَ الْعَرَبِ إيّاهُمْ ، وَعَلى الْعَرَبِ أَنْ يَعُودُوا إلى تارِيخِهِمِ الْقَدِيمِ ، لِيَأْخُذُوا مِنْهُ الْعِبْرَةَ وَالْعِظَةَ ، فَحِينما هاجَمَ التَّتارُ الْعَرَبَ لَمْ يَسْتَطِيعُوا التَّغَلُّبَ عَلَيْهِمْ ، إلاَّ بَعْدَ أَنْ اتَّحَدُوا وَوَقَفُوا صَفّاً واحِداً وَحِينَ هاجَمَ الْفِرِنْجَةُ الْعَرَبَ ، لَمْ يَسْتَطِيعُوا التَّغَلُّبَ عَلَيْهِمْ إلاَّ بِقُوَّتِهِمْ .

تَأْتَى الرِّماحُ إِذا اجْتَمعْنَ تَكَسُّراً   وَإِذا افْتَرقْنَ تَكَسَّرَتْ آحادا
إِنَّ هذا الْقَرْنَ كَغَيْرِهِ مِنَ الْقُرونِ السَّابِقَةِ لا يُجْدي فيهِ إِلاَّ
الْقُوَّةُ ، وَلا يُعيدُ الْحَقَّ الْمُغْتَصَبَ إِلاَّ الْكِفاحُ .

شَرْحُ الْمُفْرَداتِ
عَنْوَة : قَهْراً وَقَسْراً ، تَقِفُ حائِلاً : تَقِفُ حاجِزاً ، يُكَبِّدون : هنا
بمعنى يُصيبون .

أَجِبْ :
١ – ضَعْ لِكُلِّ مَقْطَعٍ عُنواناً صَغيراً .
٢ – أَيْنَ تَنْتَهي أَطْماعُ الصَّهاينةِ ؟
٣ – ما أبْرزُ أسْبابِ النَّصْرِ في التاريخِ العربيِّ ؟
٤ – لِماذا شَبَّهَ الكاتِبُ مَوْقِعَ فِلَسْطينَ من البلادِ العربيَّةِ بِمَوْقِعِ القَلْبِ من
الجَسَدِ ؟
أَلْفِظُ جَيِّداً :

أَقْرَأُ ما يلي وأُلْقِيَةِ إلى أَلْوَصْلِ بَيْنَ الكلماتِ :
بَعْدَ أَن اتَّحدوا ، باسْتِمْرارٍ ، إذا افْتَرقن .
أَقْرَأُ جَيِّداً :
أَقْرَأُ بيتَ الشِّعْرِ قِراءَةً مُعَبِّرة منتبهاً إلى عَدمِ لَفْظِ هَمْزَةِ الْوَصْلِ

—٩٦—

The Arabs must return to their ancient history and learn a lesson from it. When the Tartars attacked the Arabs they were unable to overpower them until they unified and consolidated their ranks. When the Crusaders attacked the Arabs, they were unable to defeat them. . . . In this century, as in previous ones, only power helps and only the struggle returns the stolen right.

Source: *Reader for the Sixth Grade, Part II,* 1997–1998, pp. 95–96.

الجمهورية العربية السورية
وزارة التربية

التربية الاجتماعية

السادس الابتدائي

١٤١٩هـ
١٩٩٨ـ١٩٩٩م

المؤسسة العامة للمطبوعات والكتب المدرسية

الدرس الرابع والعشرون

شهداءُ الأمة العربية «شهداءُ أمتنا»

٣ ــ شهداءُ النّضال من أجلِ تحرير جنوبيّ لبنان

لقد احتلَّ العدوُّ الاسرائيليُّ في عامِ ١٩٨٠ جنوبيَّ لبنانَ ، بدعمِ
من الولاياتِ المتحدةِ الأمريكيةِ ،والامبرياليةِ العالميةِ ، ودخلَ المدنَ
والقرى ، ليجعلَها محميةً اسرائيليةً ، يتحوَّلُ سكانُها إلى   مرتزقةٍ
يعملون تحت سيطرةِ العدوّ الإسرائيلي وينفِّذون رغباتِه ، ولكنَّ
سكانَ الجنوبِ الشرفاءَ ، العربَ المخلصينَ لوطنِهم وأرضِهم ، لم
يرتضوا ذلك ، فهبوا في وجهِ العدوّ الاسرائيلي يسحَقون خِططَهُ
العدوانية الدنيئة تحت ضرباتِ المقاومةِ الشريفةِ ، التي تمثلتْ في أبطالٍ
استشهدوا دفاعاً عن الحريةِ والكرامةِ ، يبحثون عن الشهادة في
معسكرات العدوّ و قوافِلِه ودوْريّاته .

فالبطلُ الشهيدُ نزيه قبرصلي . ابن مدينة صيدا المكافحة . شابٌّ
في مقتبَل العمر ، لم يقبلْ أن يدنِّسَ الصهاينةُ أرضَ وطنِه لبنان .
فاندفع في صبيحةِ يومٍ من الأيام إلى ساحةٍ من ساحات صيدا ،
ينتظرُ مرورَ دوريةٍ اسرائيلية ينقضُّ عليها بالقنابلِ ويفتكُ بأفرادِ العدوّ
الغاشم . وما إن مرَّت الدوريةُ الاسرائيليةُ في تلك الساحةِ ، حتى
فاجأَها نزيهٌ برصاصِ بندقيتِه الآلية . وأخذ يفتك بأفرادها ،
ويرميهم الواحد تِلْوَ الآخر ، ويقاتلهم بشرفٍ وإباءٍ ، إلى أن تمكنوا
منه واستُشْهِدَ البطلُ على أرضِ الواجبِ شهيداً مخلصاً لوطنه وبلاده
وللأمةِ العربيةِ وقضيّتِها فكان مثالاً رائعاً للبطولةِوالفداءِ .

١١٤

لقد ضحّى نزيه وكثيرون غيرُه من الأبطالِ بأرواحهم فداءً للوطن ضد الغزاة الاسرائيليين ، نزيه واحدٌ من أولئك الأبطال الذين تحدّث

عنهم الرئيسُ حافظٌ الأسد فقال : «بارك الله بكم أيها المقاومون في لبنان، باركم الله والشعبُ أيها الشهداءُ، فانتم زهراتُ الأمة، قدّمتُم المثلَ والقُدْوَةَ وعلّمتُم أن الأمةَ العربيةَ لن تستسلمَ، علَّمتُم الاسرائيليينَ أن الجماهيرَ العربيةَ أسقطتْ من حسابها الترددَ والخوفَ من دباباتهم وطائراتهم».

وهكذا ترى أن الشهادةَ طريقُ تحطيمِ العدوان ، وتحطيمِ الغزاةِ، الذين غادروا جنوبيَّ لبنان تحت ضربات المقاومةِ اللبنانيةِ الشريفةِ ، وقد لقّنهم شهداءُ لبنان درساً لا يُنسى ، وتركوا في نفوسِهِمُ الرعبَ والخوفَ ، وعادت إلى جنوبيِّ لبنانَ كرامتُه ، وحرّرَ أرضَهُ · وكما قالَ الرئيس حافظ الأسد: «لن نشعرَ بـالكرامةِ ونسعدَ بهذا الشعور إلا بقدْرِ مانشعرُ أن الشهادةَ جزءٌ لاينفصلُ من كياننا النفسي والبدني».

أسئلة الدرس :

— ما تاريخُ اجتياح العدو الاسرائيلي للقطرِ العربي اللبناني ؟
— كيف واجه أبناءُ الشعبِ اللبناني جنودَ الاحتلال ؟
— هل حققَ العدو أطماعه في لبنان ؟
— اذكر قولَ الرئيس حافظ الأسد في وصفِ الشهادة والشهيد ؟

We will feel honorable and happy only to the extent to which martyrdom becomes an inseparable part of our mental and physical existence.

Source: *Social Education for the Sixth Grade,* 1998–1999, pp. 114–15.

مطالعة :

طريق الشهادة

هذه هي طريقُ الحقِّ . هذه هي طريقُ العدلِ . هذه هي طريقُ المجدِ إنها طريقُ الشهادةِ . لأذكُرَ الآنَ أسماءَ الشهيداتِ الشبيبات والشهداءِ الشبيبيين لأنهن كثيراتٌ ولأنهم كثيرون . الإكبارُ والإجلالُ لشهداءِ الشبيبةِ شباباً وشابّات . الحب كلُّ الحبِّ لشهداءِ الشبيبةِ شباباً وشابات . المجدُ والخلود لشهداءِ الشبيبةِ شباباً وشابات . العهدُ كلُّ العهدِ لشهداءِ الشبيبةِ شباباً وشابات أن نكونَ على نفسِ الطريقِ . فالشهادةُ قيمةُ القيمِ وذمّةُ الذممِ .

لن يكون الوطن منيعاً من غير الشهادة

أيها الشبيبيون :

أنتم في طليعةِ من يجب أن يقدّسَ الشهادةَ ويحملَ رايتها . أينما كان موقعكُم : في المدرسةِ ، في الجيشِ ، في المعملِ ، في المزرعةِ ، فلن يكونَ الوطنُ منيعاً بغيرِ الشهادةِ ، ولن نصونَ حقوقنا بغيرِ الشهادةِ ، ولن نردعَ العدوانَ ونهزمَ الغزاةَ بغير الشهادة ولن نشعرَ بالكرامةِ ونسعدَ بهذا الشعورِ إلا يَقدِرِ ما نشعرُ أن الشهادةَ جزءٌ لاينفصل من كياننا النفسي والبدني ، يقدر دائماً وعفوياً أن يقودَ هذا الكيانَ بمجمله كلما اقتضى ذلك الدفاعَ عن الشعبِ والوطنِ . والشهادةُ استمرارٌ للحياةِ ، وهي الوجهُ الأنصعُ والأرحبُ لها . والشهادةُ ليست إلا نُقْلةً

١١٩

نوعيةٌ من صفحةِ الحياةِ الضيِّقة إلى صفحةِ الحياةِ الرحبةِ التي لانقتض
حدودٌ ، فالشهادةُ خلودٌ والشهيدُ خالدٌ أبداً فهو حيٌّ أبداً .

الشهادة هي الخلود

فلنعشقِ الشهادةَ مادامت هي-الخلودُ . ولنباركِ الشهداءَ . وبخذ
دربهم أمنيَّتُنا الدائمة وليكنْ زمنُنا زمنَ الشهادةِ . ولنعشْ زمنَ الشهدهه
ولنجعلْ منه زمناً شعبياً عربياً يُخْلَقُ فيه الإنسانُ الجديدُخالياً من الحقد
والشوائبَ . متحرراً من الخوفِ والأنانيةِ والجشعِ . فينحصر
العدوانُ . ويتحطمُ الغزاةُ . ويتحطمُ الاستعمارُ والهيمنةُ .
وينهار الظلمُ هنا وفي كلِّ مكانٍ ، ومن يعشْ زمنَ الشهادةِ يكنس
الظلمَ في كلِّ مكانٍ .

ونحن نتحدثُ عن الشهادةِ نذكرُ بفخرٍ واعتزازٍ أولئك الأبطال. من
أرضِ لبنانَ العربي ، الذين يجسدون الشهادةَ . والذينَ آمنوا أ.
الشهادةَ هي الطريقُ لطردِ الغزو وتأديبِ الغزاةِ الاسرائيليين سسه.
تصوّروا أنهم سيقضَمون ماشاؤوا من أرضِ لبنانَ وسيحوّلون مابسقى
من لبنانَ إلى محميةٍ اسرائيلية يتحوّلُ ساكنوها إلى شراذمَ من المرتزقه .
فخابَ أملُهم أسوأَ خيبةٍ ، وسُحِقتْ خططهم العدوانية الدنيئة ، حت
ضرباتِ الأبطالِ المقاومين الذين تحولوا إلى أمواجٍ عارمةٍ م
المستشهدين الذين يبحثون عن الشهادة ليمارسوها ، حيث يوجدُ الحسء
في معسكرات الإسرائيليين ، وفي مخافرِ الإسرائيليين ، وفي ئه عاه
الإسرائيليين وأماكنِ تواجدِ الدوريات الإسرائيلية .

١٢٠

[We] admire and respect the young male and female martyrs, [we give] absolute love [to them]. . . . [We pledge] full commitment to the young male and female martyrs to follow their path. The *Shahadah* is the supreme value. . . .

You are at the forefront of those who must sanctify the *Shahadah* and carry its flag. . . . The *Shahadah* is an inseparable part of our physical and mental entity and it can lead it altogether. . . . The *Shahadah* is the continuation of life and life's most noble and pure form. The *Shahadah* is merely a qualitative transformation from one chapter of narrow life to a much broader unlimited life. The *Shahadah* is eternity and the martyr is eternal and alive forever and ever.

Source: *Social Education for the Sixth Grade,* 1998–1999, pp. 119–20.

بوركت جماهير المقاومة اللبنانية البطلة

بارك اللّهُ بكم أيها المقاومون في لبنانَ . باركَكُم الله والشعبُ أيها الشهداءُ . فأنتم زهراتُ هذه الأمةِ . قدّمتم المَثلَ والقدوةَ . وعلّمتم أن الأمةَ العربيةَ لن تستلمَ . علّمتموهم أن السياسيين العربَ المتخاذلين ، المهزومين من داخلِ نفوسهم لايُمثلون الجماهيرَ العربيةَ . علمتموهم أن الذين يساومونهم ويطأطئون رؤوسهم أمامَ الجلادِ الإسرائيلي . إنما يفعلون ذلك خوفاً على مناصبهم وامتيازاتهم وأموالهم التي سرقوها من عرقِ الشعوبِ ، ودماءِ الشعوبِ علمتموهم أن هؤلاء ليسوا إلا عيونَالهم في صفوفنا وخونةً لجماهيرنا وسوف نحاسبهم بقسوةٍ لاتقِلُّ عن قسوتنا تجاه الغزاة . ولكن بأسلوبٍ آخرَ يليقُ بعملاءِ العدوّ في صفوفِ الشعبِ .

علّمتم الاسرائيليين أن الجماهيرَ العربيةَ أسقطت من حسابها الترّددَ والخوفَ من دباباتهم وطائراتهم . علمتموهم أن طريقَ كامب ديفيد 'وما شابهها ليست ·إلا طريقَ الموتِ الحياني لمن يتطلعُ إليه ويسيرُ عليه .

أيها المقاومون في لبنان .

إن سوريةَ معكم قولاً وفعلاً وستظلُّ على استعدادٍ لأن تقتسمَ معكم كلَّ شيء . ولكم في سوريةَ كما لأبناءِ سوريةَ تماماً . فالخندقُ واحدٌ . والعدوُّ واحدٌ . والمصيرُ واحدٌ .

١٢١

Oh martyrs . . . you taught [the Israelis] that the defeatist Arab politicians who have defeated souls do not represent the Arab public. You taught them that those who negotiate with them and bow their heads in front of the Israeli executioner do so out of fear for their jobs, their privileges and their money—which they stole from the sweat and blood of the people. You taught them that these are but spies in our midst and traitors of our public. And we will repay them with a harshness that is not less severe than our ruthlessness toward the invaders, but in somewhat different ways that are fit for the agents of the enemy [who are present within] our people. . . . You taught them that the path of Camp David, and other similar paths, are the paths of traitorous death for those who aspire toward and walk them.

Source: *Social Education for the Sixth Grade,* 1998–1999, p. 121.

الجمهورية العربية السورية
وزارة التربية

التربية الإسلامية

١٤١٩هـ
١٩٩٨ـ١٩٩٩م

الرابع الابتدائي

المؤسسة العامة للمطبوعات والكتب المدرسية

الصَّفْقةُ الرّابحة

تمهيد :

إنَّ الجهادَ فريضةٌ على المسلمينَ حتى لَوْ كانَ الأعداءُ أضعافَ عددِهم . وإنَّهم مَنصورونَ بعونِ اللَّهِ عَلى أعْدائِهم . فحسْبُ المؤمنينَ أنْ يُعدُّوا ما استطاعوا من القُوى وأن يَثِقوا بِنصرِ اللَّهِ .

قال اللَّه تعالى :

﴿ إنَّ اللَّهَ اشترىٰ مِنَ المؤمنينَ أَنْفُسَهُمْ وأموالَهمْ بأنَّ لهمُ الجَنَّةَ يُقاتِلونَ في سبيلِ اللَّهِ فَيَقْتُلونَ ويُقْتَلونَ وَعْداً عليه حَقًّا في التَّوراةِ والإنجيلِ والقرآنِ ومَنْ أَوْفَ بِعَهْدِهِ مِنَ اللَّهِ فاستبشِروا بِبَيعِكُمُ الذي بايَعتُم بِهِ وذلك هوَ الفَوْزُ العظيمُ . ﴾

شرح المفردات :

حقًّا :	لازماً .
التوراة :	الكتاب الذي أنزله اللَّهُ على موسى عليه السلام .
الإنجيل :	الكتاب الذي أنزله الله على عيسى عليه السلام .

المعنى العام :

يتضمَّن هذا النَّصُ ما يلي :

لقد باعَ المؤمنونَ المُجاهدونَ أنْفُسَهُمْ لِلَّهِ ، وَبَذَلوا أرواحَهُمْ في سبيلِ اللهِ . فدافعوا عن عقيدتِهم وأوْطانِهم بِقوّةٍ وشجاعةٍ . فَقتلوا الأعداءَ الكثيرينَ . وَقُتِلوا في سَبيلِ اللهِ فكانوا شُهداءَ خالدين . واستحقُّوا بذلك جنّةَ اللهِ ورِضْوانَهُ يَوْمَ القيامةِ .

جميعُ الشَّرائعِ الدِّينيةِ وكلُّ الكُتبِ السّماويةِ أكَّدَتْ أنَّ الشُّهداءَ مُكَرَّمونَ عندَ اللهِ عَزَّ وجلَّ . وقد وَعَدَهُم اللهُ بالثوابِ العظيمِ والأجْرِ الكريمِ . واللهُ لايُخْلِفُ المِيعادَ .

هذه البشرى العظيمةُ يَزُفُّها اللهُ سُبْحانَهُ إلى المُجاهدينَ الأبطالِ لتطمئنَّ قُلوبُهم وترتاحَ ضمائِرُهُم فَيَنْدَفِعونَ إلى المعركةِ من غيرِ خَوْفٍ ولاتَرَدُّدٍ ، مُؤمنينَ بِقَوْلِ رسولِ اللهِ ﷺ « تَكَفَّلَ اللهُ لِمنْ خَرَجَ في سبيله لايُخْرِجُهُ إلاّ جهادٌ في سبيلي وتصديقٌ بِرُسُلي بأنْ تَوَفّاهُ أنْ يُدْخِلَهُ الجنةَ أو يُرجِعَهُ إلى منزلِهِ الذي خَرَجَ منه نائلاً مانالَ من أُجْرٍ أو غَنيمةٍ .. » ولذلك فهم مُصمِّمونَ مُصِرُّونَ على إدراكِ إحدى الحُسْنَيَيْنِ ، النَّصرِ أو الشَّهادةِ وهذا هو النّجاحُ العظيمُ في الدّنيا والآخرةِ .

الإرشادُ والتّوجيهُ :

١ ــ اشترى اللهُ عَزَّ وجلَّ من المؤمنين أنْفُسَهم وأموالَهم بأن لهم الجنةَ فَقَبِلَ المؤمنون ذلك وتمَّتِ المُبايَعَةُ عن رضىً وطَواعيةٍ فاستحقُّوا الثَّمن الغالي وهو الجنةُ والثوابُ العظيمُ .

٢ ـــ للمجاهدين الصّامدين الذين يَقْتُلون الأعداءَ ويُقتلون في سبيلِ اللّه الثَّوابُ العظيمُ عندَ اللّه تعالى .

٣ ـــ جميعُ الكتبِ السّماويّةِ أقرّتْ عظيمَ ثوابِ الشّهيدِ ووعدَت به .

٤ ـــ إنَّ اللّهَ سُبحانَهُ لايُخلفُ الميعادَ .

الأسئلة والمناقشة :

١ ـــ ما الثمن الذي اشترى به اللّه تعالى أنْفُسَ المؤمنين وأموالهم ؟

٢ ـــ وَعَدَ اللّهُ عزَّ وَجَلَّ المجاهدين الصّابرين والشهداء بالثَّواب العظيم . اكتب الآية التي تُثبِتُ ذلك واحفظها .

٣ ـــ قالَ عليهِ السّلام : من قاتَلَ لتكون كلمةُ اللّه هي العليا فهو في سبيلِ اللّهِ : اكتب من الآية المقطع الذي يُؤيّدُ هذا المعنى ويحددُ الغاية من الجهادِ .

٤ ـــ بَيْعُ المؤمنين أنْفُسَهم وأموالهم للّه تعالى تجارةٌ رابحةٌ وبشارةٌ عظيمةٌ . اكتب من النص المقطع الذي يتحدّث عن ذلك .

Allah has bought from the believers their souls and their properties for they shall inherit Paradise, they will fight for the cause of *Allah* and they will kill [the enemies] and will be killed. This is a promise *Allah* took upon Himself in the Torah, the New Testament, and *The Koran.* . . . Rejoice in the deal you made with Him.

Source: *Islamic Education for the Fourth Grade,* 1998–1999, pp. 44–46.

الجمهورية العربية السورية
وزارة التربية

التّربية الإسلاميّة

١٤١٩هـ
١٩٩٨-١٩٩٩م

السّادس الابتدائي

المؤسسة العامة للمطبوعات والكتب المدرسية

وإلى المسجدِ الأقصى ، كانَ إسراءُ رسولِنا محمد صلَّى اللهُ عليه وسلَّمَ من مكة .

وفي المسجد الأقصى ، صلَّى رسولُنا محمدٌ صلَّى اللهُ عليه وسلَّمَ إماماً بالأنبياء في ليلةِ الإسراءِ .

ومن المسجدِ الأقصى كانَ عُروجُ رسولِنا محمد صلى اللهُ عليه وسلَّمَ إلى السماءِ ليتلقَّى كلماتِ اللهِ . . .

وإلى المسجدِ الأقصى كانَتْ قِبلةُ المسلمين في كلِّ صلاة قبلَ أن يجعلَ اللهُ الكعبةَ قِبلتَهُم في كلِّ صلاة .

في المسجدِ الأقصى يُضاعِفُ اللهُ ثوابَ العبادةِ أضعافاً كثيرةً .

اليهودُ أعداءُ اللهِ يريدون أن يَبقُوا في فلسطينَ ، لِيَستَولُوا على المسجدِ الأقصى .

الدفاعُ عن المسجدِ الأقصى فرضٌ على كلِّ مسلم ومسلمةٍ لأنَّ اللهَ طهَّرَهُ ، وباركَ حولَهُ ، فلا يجوزُ أن يُدنسَهُ أعداءُ اللهِ .

المسلمونَ في بلادِ الدنيا يكافحون لإجلاء اليهودِ عن فلسطينَ ، دِفاعا عن المسجدِ الأقصى . . .

لا عُثْرَ ولا مغفرةَ لمن يقعدُ عن الجهادِ في سبيلِ اللهِ لتطهير فلسطينَ من اليهودِ .

تطهيرُ فلسطينَ من اليهودِ دفاعاً عن المسجدِ الأقصى جهادٌ في سبيلِ اللهِ .

هو أولُ بيتٍ للهِ

أرضِ فلسطينَ .

تُ مريمَ العذراءِ

، فبشَّرها بميلادِ

ولَ اليهودُ أعداءُ

— ٥٧ —

المسلمونَ في كلِّ أقطارِ الدُّنيا· يستعدونَ لجهادِ اليهودِ وطردِهم مِن فلسطينَ.

نحنُ نستعدُّ لجهادِ اليهودِ وطردِهم من فلسطينَ الحبيبةِ.

ما أحلى الموتَ في سبيلِ اللهِ.

الذينَ يموتونَ في سبيلِ اللهِ أحياءٌ عِندَ ربِّهم في الجنةِ.

❂ ❂ ❂

Muslims throughout the world struggle to expel the Jews from Palestine and to protect the Al-Aqsa Mosque. There is no forgiveness for whoever avoids the *Jihad* in the cause of *Allah* for the purification of Palestine from the Jews. The purification of Palestine from the Jews in order to protect the Al-Aqsa Mosque is a *Jihad* for *Allah*.

Muslims throughout the world are preparing for *Jihad* against the Jews and for their expulsion from Palestine. . . .

It is so wonderful to die for *Allah*.

Those who die for the cause of *Allah*, live with their God in Paradise.

Source: *Islamic Education for the Sixth Grade*, 1998–1999, pp. 57–58.

الجمهورية العربية السورية
وزارة التربية

التربية الإسلامية

الثالث الإعدادي

١٤٢٠هـ ــ ١٩٩٩ــ٢٠٠٠م

المؤسسة العامة للمطبوعات والكتب المدرسية

فخرج الرسول صلى الله عليه وسلم ومعه جميع من حضر من خلص المؤمنين •
وكانوا (٦٣٠) فأقام النبي عليه الصلاة والسلام بحمراء الأسد (على بعد ثمانيــة
أميال من المدينة) ثلاثة أيام • فلم يلق أبا سفيان ، وألقى الله في قلبه الرعب ، ثم
رجعوا مصحوبين (بنعمة الله) وهي السلامة مع إذلال العدو بإرغامه على الفرار ،
(وفضل) : وهو الأجر العظيم في الآخرة والربح من التجارة ، فإن الرسول صلى الله
عليه وسلم اشترى إبلا وباعها فربح مالا فقسمه بين أصحابه •

إنهم عادوا بخير الدنيا والآخرة ولم يصبهم أذى على الرغم من لقائهم العدو
تنفيذا لأمر الله وابتغاء مرضاته • وعظيم فضلــه • (واتبعوا رضوان الله والله ذو
فضل عظيم) •

ولقد حاول شياطين الإنس من المنافقين أن يرهبوا المؤمنين ويثبطوا عزائمهـم
عن حرب عدوهم فقالوا لهم « إن الناس قد جمعوا لكم فاخشوهم » فثبّت الله
قلوب المؤمنين ، إذ بين لهم أن هؤلاء الأعداء عباد ضعفاء فلا تخافوهم وخافوني
أنا الله رب العالمين القادر القاهر والأمر كله بيدي إن كنتم مؤمنين •

ما ترشد اليه الآيات :

١ ــ الحث على الجهاد والترغيب فيه • لما له من ثواب عظيم في الجنة • وإيماناً
من الرئيس حافظ الأسد بمنزلة الشهداء وتكريمـاً لهم فقد أولى أسَرَهُمْ
وأطفالهم عناية كبيرة • وأقام لهم مدينة أبناء الشهداء يتلقون فيهــا العلم
ويعوضون عما فقدوه من عطف آبائهم وحنان أمهاتهم •

٢ ــ ان الاستشهاد في الحقيقة ، انتقال إلى حياة أخرى نقية ومبرأة من الهم والحزن
والأكدار • والأذى ، أي في جنات النعيم • وإن كان في ظاهره موت وانقطاع
عن الحيـاة •

٣ ــ إن الشهداء بما ينعمون به في جنات الخلد • يأملون أن يقدم إخوانهم في الدنيا
على الجهاد • ويستشهدوا • وينالوا رضا الله تعالى •

Martyrdom is, in fact, a transition to another life that is refined and pure from all worries and sorrows. . . . The martyrs, through their overwhelming joy in the Hereafter, wish that their brothers in [this] world would wage *Jihad*, become martyrs themselves, and win *Allah*'s good will.

Source: *Islamic Education for the Ninth Grade,* 1999–2000, p. 41.

الجمهورية العربية السورية
وزارة التربية

القراءة

الجزء الأول

الخامس الابتدائي

١٤١٩ هـ ـ ١٩٩٨ ـ ١٩٩٩ م
المؤسسة العامة للمطبوعات والكتب المدرسية

القِراءَة

اَلْفِدائِيُّ الصَّغِيرُ

– في أَحَدِ مُعَسْكَراتِ الأَشْبالِ مِنْ أَبْناءِ فِلَسْطينَ، يَتَدَرَّبُ أَيْهَمُ عَلَى حَمْلِ السِّلاحِ وَيَسْتَعِدُّ هُوَ وَرِفاقُهُ الصِّغارُ لِلْمُشارَكَةِ في تَحْرير بَلَدِهِ.

يَقِفُ الْمُدَرِّبُ أَمامَ صِغارِهِ الأَشْبالِ كُلَّ يَوْمٍ، يُحَدِّثُهُمْ مِنْ أَعْماقِ قَلْبِهِ، فَيَقولُ: يا أَبْنائي، هَذِهِ الْخِيامُ التي تَعيشونَ فيها الْيَوْمَ، لَيْسَتْ مَنازِلَكُمْ،

إنَّ بيوتَكُمْ هُناكَ ، في الأَرْضِ المُحْتَلَّةِ ، وَرَاءَ هَذِهِ الجِبالِ كانَ لِكُلِّ واحِدٍ مِنكُمْ أَرْضٌ ، أَوْمَنْزِلٌ ، أَوْبَيَّارَةٌ ، ثم جَاءَ العَدُوُّ الصِهِيَوْنِيُّ ، فَطَرَدَ أَهْلَكُم مِنها بِقُوَّةِ السِلاحِ نَحْنُ نَكْرَهُ الحَرْبَ ، ولكِنَّنا نَكْرَهُ أَيْضاً أَنْ نَعيشَ مُشَرَّدِينَ تَحْتَ سَمْعِ العَالَمِ وَبصَرِهِ .

- سَيَتَعَلَّمُ أَطْفالُ المُخَيِّماتِ استِخْدامَ الأَسْلِحَةِ الخَفيفةِ ، وَيَتَدَرَّبُونَ عَلَى مَعاركِ السِلاحِ الأَبْيَضِ ، وَيَفْرَحُ مُدَرِّبُهُم حينَ يَراهُم يُتْقِنُونَ فُنُونَ القِتالِ ، مِثْلَما يَحْفَظُونَ دُروسَهُمْ.

- في ذَلِكَ اليَوْمِ ، زارَ المُعَسْكَرَ وَفدٌ مِنَ السَّيداتِ العَرَبيَّاتِ ، فَقَدَّمْنَ لِلأَشْبالِ مَلابِس شِتائِيَّةً نَسَجْنَها لَهُمْ ، وكتَبَتْ كُلُّ سَيِّدةٍ رِسالَةً إِلى الصِغارِ مَعَ الهَدِيَّةِ . قَرأَ أَيْهَمُ رِسالَةَ السَّيِّدَةِ العَرَبيَّةِ التي نَسَجَتْ لَهُ هَدِيَّتَهُ فَإِذَا فيها :

أَيُّها الشِبْلُ الصَّغيرُ ! نَسَجْتُها لَكَ مِنْ خُيوطِ الأَمَلِ ، أَمَلِ شَعبِنا الكَبيرِ بِكَ ، فَقاتِلْ ، فَإِنَّ الوَرْدَ يَنْبُتُ مِنَ الجِراحِ ، قاتِلْ حَتَى تأْخُذَني مَعَكَ إِلى بَلَدِي فِلَسْطِينَ .

٤ - بَعَثَتْ رِسَالَةُ السَّيِّدَةِ الدِّفءَ في نَفْسِ أَيْهَمَ ، بِمِقدَارِ ماأَدْفَأَتْهُ حَرارَةُ اللِّباسِ الصُّوفِيِّ الَّذي نَسَجَتْهُ يَدُهَا ، فَأَقْبَلَ عَلَى

التَّدَرُّبِ وَهُوَ أَكْثَرُ ثِقَةً وَأَشَدُّ إِيمَاناً بِحَقِّ شَعْبِهِ فِي الحَيَاةِ .

في كُلِّ عامٍ يَتَخَرَّجُ في مُعَسْكَرَاتِ الثَّوْرَةِ الفِلَسْطِينِيَّةِ أَفْوَاجٌ مِنَ الأَشْبَالِ ، وَتَمُرُّ الأَيَّامُ ، فَإِذا هُمْ يَكْبَرُونَ ، وَيَقُودونَ عملياتٍ فِدائِيَّةً جَرِيئَةً ، يَنْقَضُّونَ على العَدُوِّ ، فَيَنْسِفونَ دَبَّابَاتِهِ ومُصَفَّحَاتِهِ ، وَيَبْعَثُونَ الرُّعْبَ في نُفُوسِ جُنودِهِ ، حَتَّى يَقْتَنِعَ في آخِرِ الأَمْرِ أَنَّ الغَاصِبَ لابَقَاءَ لَهُ ، وَأَنَّ الأَرْضَ لأَصْحَابِها .

شَرْحُ المُفْرَدَاتِ

الأَشْبَالُ : جَمْعُ شِبْلٍ ، وَهُوَ وَلَدُ الأَسَدِ ، البَيَّارَةُ : مَزْرَعَةُ البُرْتُقَالِ

أُجِيبُ

١ -- لِماذا يتدَرَّبُ أَيْهَمُ على حَمْلِ السِّلاحِ ؟

٢ -- ماذا يَكْرَهُ الفِلَسْطِينِيونَ العَرَبُ ؟

٣ -- مابَرْنامَجُ أَطْفَالِ المُخَيَّمَاتِ في المُعَسْكَرِ ؟

٤ -- ضَعْ عُنْواناً مناسِباً لِلمَقْطَعِ الثالِثِ .

٥ - كَيْفَ أَقْبَلَ أَيْهَمُ على التدرُّبِ ؟

٦ -- مامَعْنَى عبارةِ : الأَرْضُ لأَصْحَابِها ؟

In one of the camps of the young Sons of Palestine, Ayham is training in carrying weapons and he and his little friends are preparing to participate in the liberation of their country. . . .

The children in the camps learn to use light weapons and fight with cold weapons. Their instructor is pleased to see that they learn the martial arts just as they learn their [regular] lessons. . . . Each year, regiments of youth come out from the camps of the Palestinian revolution. Time passes and they grow up and lead courageous *Fedai* operations, defeat the enemy, set fire to his tanks and armored cars, and terrorize the enemy soldiers' hearts, until the enemy ultimately realizes that the plunderer will not survive and the land belongs to its owner.

Source: *Reader for the Fifth Grade, Part I,* 1998–1999, pp. 109–11.

الجمهورية العربية السورية
وزارة التربية

التربية الإسلامية

الثاني الثانوي

١٤٢٠هـ ــ ١٩٩٩ ــ ٢٠٠٠م
المؤسسة العامة للمطبوعات والكتب المدرسية

شرح المفردات:

من الذين هادوا: جماعة من اليهود. **اسمع غير مسمع:** اسمع لا أسمعك الله.
راعنا: راعنا سمعك ويقصدون الرعونة والسب. **ليّاً بالسنتهم:** فتلاً بها
وانحرافاً. **نطمس وجوهاً.** نمحوها ونفسدها. **فنردها على أدبارها:** نجعلها كالأقفاء
شكلاً واحداً. **فتيلاً:** يضرب مثلاً للقلة وهو الخيط الذي في شق النواة. **الجبت:**
الأصنام. **الطاغوت:** يطلق على كل من دعا إلى الطغيان والضلالة. **نقيراً:** النقرة في
ظهر النواة يضرب للقلة. **ظليلاً:** صفة مشتقة من الظل إي ظلاً وارفاً دائماً.

الإرشاد والتوجيه:

١ـ إن اليهود لا يألون جهداً في إضلالنا وعدائنا وتكذيب رسولنا الكريم
والتأليب ضدنا وتحريف الكتب السماوية.

٢ـ الكتب السماوية في أصلها تدعو إلى الإيمان بالله والعمل الصالح.

٣ـ من رحمته تعالى أنه يغفر الذنوب جميعا لمن أتاه تائباً مستغفراً إلا الشرك.

٤ـ اليهود يتعاونون مع المشركين والملحدين ضد المسلمين لأنهم يرون في
الإسلام كشفاً لأساليبهم الماكرة وأخلاقهم الشريرة.

٥ـ من أسباب عداوة اليهود للعرب أن الله بعث محمداً خاتم النبيين من العرب
وكانوا يعتقدون أن النبوة مقصورة عليهم، فيندفعون وراء عنصريتهم في زعمهم
أنهم صفوة الخلق والمقربون من الله. قالوا: ﴿ نحن أبناء الله وأحباؤه ﴾   "المائدة
١٨" وقولهم: ﴿ لن يدخل الجنة إلا من كان هوداً أو نصارى﴾   "البقرة ١١١".

٦ـ علينا أن نعمل الصالحات ونتدبر آيات الله كي يكرمنا الله، وإن الكتاب
الإلهي وحده لا يتحرك لإنهاض أمة مهما نال هذا الكتاب من تقديس وإجلال،

The Jews spare no effort to deceive us, hate us, deny our Prophet, incite against us, and distort the holy scriptures. The Jews cooperate with the Polytheist and the infidels against the Muslims because they know Islam reveals their crafty ways and abject characteristics. One of the reasons for the Jews' hostility to the Arabs is that *Allah* sent Muhammad, the last of the prophets, from amongst the Arabs, while they thought prophecy was solely their domain.

Source: *Islamic Education for the Eleventh Grade,* 1999–2000, p. 33.

الجمهورية العربية السورية
وزارة التربية

الأول الثانوي

أ

التربية الإسلامية

١٤٢٠هـ ــ ١٩٩٩ــ ٢٠٠٠م

المؤسسة العامة للمطبوعات والكتب المدرسية

لذلك فإن منطق العدالة الصحيح يوجب فيهم حكماً واحداً لامفر من تنفيذه . هو أن يرد قصدهم الإجرامي عليهم باستئصالهم .

وماعلى المسلمين في عصرنا ـ واليهود جاثمون في ديارهم وأرضهم المقدسة ـ إلا أن يجمعوا أمرهم ويوحدوا صفوفهم ويناجزوا عدوهم الحرب حتى يحكم الله بيننا وبينهم قال تعالى : «ولينصرن الله من ينصره . إن الله لقوي عزيز» الحج : ٤٠

الإرشاد والتوجيه :

١ ــ رسول الله صلى الله عليه وسلم هو القدوة الحسنة الصالحة للمسلمين في حربهم وسلمهم .

٢ ــ على المسلم أن يعاهد ربه على الجهاد في سبيل الله وأن يفي بهذا العهد .

٣ ــ الشدائد لاتزيد المؤمنين إلا قوة وصبراً وإيماناً بالله وتسليما له .

٤ ــ مكافأة المؤمنين الصادقين على صدقهم وعذاب المنافقين على نفاقهم .

٥ ــ قوة الله لاتقهر وعزته لاتغلب . ورحمة الله واسعة لمن تاب من ذنبه ورجع إلى ربه .

مناقشة وتطبيقات

١ ــ ما موقف اليهود من العهود في التاريخ ؟

٢ ــ ما موقف قريش من خيانة اليهود للمسلمين ؟

٣ ــ ما الخطة العسكرية الغريبة التي فاجأ بها المسلمون قريشاً في المدينة ؟

٤ ــ كيف انتهت معركة الأحزاب ؟

٥ ــ ما العبرة التي تستخلصها من هذه الغزوة ؟

٦ ــ ما مهمة نعيم بن مسعود في هذه المعركة ؟ وكيف حققها ؟

٧ ــ هل كان قتل رجال بني قريظة ظلماً أم عدلاً . ولماذا ؟

الوظيفة :

ارجع إلى أحد الكتب التي تبحث في تاريخ اليهود ولخص موقفهم من الإسلام والمسلمين .

"The logic of justice," concludes the book, "obligates the application of the single verdict [on the Jews] from which there is no escape; namely, that their criminal intentions be turned against them and that they be exterminated. The duty of Muslims of our time is to pull themselves together, unite their ranks, and wage war on their enemy until *Allah* hands down his judgment on them and us."

Source: *Islamic Education for the Tenth Grade,* 1999–2000, p. 116.

Bibliography

Note: All books were published by the Syrian Ministry of Education and printed by the General Institute for Schoolbook Printing.

1. *Reader for the Fourth Grade, Part I.* 1999–2000.
2. *Reader for the Fifth Grade, Part I.* 1998–1999.
3. *Reader for the Fifth Grade, Part II.* 1998–1999.
4. *Reader for the Sixth Grade, Part I.* 1999–2000.
5. *Reader for the Sixth Grade, Part II.* 1999–2000.
6. *Reader and Literature for the Seventh Grade.* 1999–2000.
7. *Language and Literature for the Tenth Grade.* 1997–1998.
8. *Language and Literature for the Eleventh Grade* (Humanities Section). 1999–2000.
9. *Language and Literature for the Eleventh Grade* (Science Section). 1999–2000.
10. *Reader and Literature for the Ninth Grade.* 1999–2000.
11. *Ancient History of the Arabs for the Fifth Grade.* 1998–1999.
12. *History—The Era of the Prophet and the Righteous Caliphs, for the Sixth Grade.* 1999–2000.
13. *History of the Arabs in the Umayyad Era for the Seventh Grade.* 1999–2000.
14. *History of the Arabs in the Abbasid Era for the Seventh Grade.* 1999–2000.

15. *Modern History of the Arabs for the Ninth Grade.* 1999–2000.
16. *History of the Arab Civilization for the Tenth Grade.* 1999–2000.
17. *Social Education for the Fourth Grade.* 1998–1999.
18. *Social Education for the Fifth Grade.* 1997–1998.
19. *Social Education for the Sixth Grade.* 1998–1999.
20. *National (Pan-Arab) Socialist Education for the Seventh Grade.* 1999–2000.
21. *National (Pan-Arab) Socialist Education for the Eighth Grade.* 1999–2000.
22. *National (Pan-Arab) Socialist Education for the Ninth Grade.* 1999–2000.
23. *National (Pan-Arab) Socialist Education for the Tenth Grade.* 1998–1999.
24. *National (Pan-Arab) Socialist Education for the Eleventh Grade.* 1999–2000.
25. *Islamic Education for the Fourth Grade.* 1998–1999.
26. *Islamic Education for the Fifth Grade.* 1998–1999.
27. *Islamic Education for the Sixth Grade.* 1998–1999.
28. *Islamic Education for the Seventh Grade.* 1999–2000
29. *Islamic Education for the Ninth Grade.* 1999–2000.
30. *Islamic Education for the Tenth Grade.* 1999–2000.
31. *Islamic Education for the Eleventh Grade.* 1999–2000.
32. *Geography of Syria (Bilad Al-Sham[1]) for the Fifth Grade.* 1999–2000.
33. *Geography of the Arab Homeland for the Sixth Grade.* 1998–1999.
34. *Geography of the Syrian Arab (Qutr) for the Eighth Grade.* 1999–2000.
35. *Geography of the Arab Homeland for the Ninth Grade.* 1999–2000.
36. *Natural Geography for the Tenth Grade.* 1999–2000.
37. *Geography of the World for the Eleventh Grade.* 1999–2000.

1. *Bilad Al-Sham* included, historically, Syria, Lebanon, Trans-Jordan, and Palestine.